INFLATION

Other books by Robert Lekachman

The Age of Keynes
National Income and the Public Welfare

Robert Lekachman

INFLATION
The Permanent Problem of Boom and Bust

VINTAGE BOOKS NEW YORK

A Division of Random House

Vintage Books Edition, September 1973
Copyright © 1973 by Robert Lekachman
All rights reserved under International and Pan-American Copyright Conventions. Published in the United States by Random House, Inc., New York, and simultaneously in Canada by Random House of Canada Limited, Toronto.

Library of Congress Cataloging in Publication Data

Lekachman, Robert.
Inflation: the permanent problem of boom and bust.
1. Inflation (Finance)—United States.   2. United
States—Economic conditions—1961–   I. Title.
[HG538.L45 1973b]   332.4'1   73–9092
ISBN 0–394–71987–5 (pbk.)

Manufactured in the United States of America

Contents

INFLATION

I.

The Process

As a chronic affliction of organized societies, inflation is fueled by private greed, the cowardice and stupidity of public men, specific characteristics of corporate and union organization, and systematic aggression by nation states. Our narrative gives due attention to each inflationary element. Since its roots are deep in the human psyche, inflation is completely controllable only at the price of considerable transformations in behavior and institutional arrangement. Much will subsequently be said about the costs, benefits, and general feasibility of available anti-inflationary strategies. Suffice it to note at the outset that the usual remedies for inflation entail unemployment, idle factories, and general recession. The wilder the inflation the deeper the recession.

War and inflation are particularly old friends.

Of human activities, wars are by far the most wasteful. Huge armies and navies are mobilized, 11.5 million men and women at the peak of the American World War II effort. Hordes of factory workers, recruited from civilian factories, the unemployment rolls, kitchens, classrooms, and old folks' homes, toil to fabricate expensive fire-crackers for the armed services to detonate. Regiments of bureaucrats, lawyers, accountants, statisticians, and economists endeavor to control prices, extract from the patriotic citizenry their savings for war-bond purchases, direct businessmen into vital, wartime activities, ration scanty stocks of clothing, meat, sugar, coffee, and gaso-line, and prosecute a high enough percentage of the black marketeers to prevent breakdown of the control system.

Needless to say, everybody is paid—soldiers, sailors, welders, lawyers, bureaucrats, civilian as well as war workers. When granted income, trained modern con-sumers desire to spend it. Anxious sellers and advertis-ers do their best to stimulate this urge. In normal circum-stances, consumer purchases are the elixir on which economic prosperity, adequate profit, and further ex-pansion depend.

War changes the rules. Ordinary people earn much larger incomes as the labor force expands, overtime becomes routine, and wage rates are bid up by labor-starved airplane, tank, and munitions plants, all operat-ing on cost-plus contracts. But at the same time, the warlike activities which generate the wages and salaries gobble up the raw materials which otherwise would be incorporated into the autos, appliances, furniture, pro-cessed foods, and other items for which people endure the tedium of routine labor.

A major war converts the federal government into a major purchaser. Thus in 1940 Washington spent a round $10 billion, a coincidental 10 percent of Gross National Product. Four years later, the figure had swelled to $95.5 billion, a plump 45.4 percent of Gross National Product. Even the Korean conflict, a much smaller American commitment, had a substantial impact upon the national budget. In 1950, federal spending totaled $40.8 billion, a bit over 14 percent of GNP, but by 1953 the comparable numbers were $77 billion and 21.1 percent.

Washington spending is speedily translated into larger incomes for the men and women who directly or indirectly get those green Treasury checks. When Detroit shuts down the auto assembly lines and converts to tanks and bombers, what are the defense workers to do with their new money? Some of it they can spend on those goods which the administrators of the war economy permit to be produced for civilian necessity and diversion. When a war boom follows hard upon the heels of protracted depression and unemployment, the newly employed can pay debts, take houses out of hock, and replenish frayed wardrobes. Finally, both because so many consumer goods are unavailable and because it is the patriotic course of action, they can save their money until final victory legitimates a glorious buying binge.

All this said, it remains likely that far too many dollars will chase far too few goods. In the absence of government intervention, prices soar, unions demand and receive protection against the escalating costs of living, corporations treat higher labor costs as sufficient reason to charge still higher prices, and the unions in response administer still a further twist to the inflationary spiral.

Once on this spiral, neither unions nor businessmen can readily dismount. The leaders of both interests realize that their price and wage gains are illusory. They know them to be also essential if employees and their employers are to avoid falling still further behind rising prices or rising costs. The public-spirited union which restrains its wage demands contributes unnoticeably to general price control unless other unions emulate its behavior. As is the usual fate of the public-spirited, the members of the "responsible" union will be unmistakably worse off than fellow workers who belong to greedier

organizations which have pressed for everything an inflationary market will bear.

Employers are in much the same boat. What avails it
that even a sizable supermarket chain vows to hold the
price line if other businessmen are busy marking up everything in sight? The patriotic supermarketeer will soon
be out of merchandise, unable to replace his depleted
inventories at higher prices, and shortly bankrupt. Thus
the efforts of individual businessmen, unions, and employees to protect themselves against inflation are not
only unavailing but the cause of still more inflation and
still more anguished efforts to catch up. Yet, failure to
compete in the inflationary race is tantamount to sharper
reductions in standards of living for wage earners, and
unacceptable erosion of profit margins for those who
hire them.

Inevitably governments which make war try to soothe
the economic fevers which accompany them. As a matter
of arithmetic, it ought to be possible to collect in new
taxes amounts large enough to pay for the upkeep of the
armed services and their civilian auxiliaries, as well as for
their arms and accouterments. A spartan government
which adopted this policy would leave civilians just
enough of their income to buy at existing prices what the
civilian economy was permitted to produce. Or, as John
Maynard Keynes advocated in 1939, the money might be
acquired by government in the shape of forced savings
to be released at the end of the war as a stimulus to
economic reconversion. It is attractively direct to extract
the $80 billion required to finance a year of war from the
citizens who endorse that endeavor.

Real life is harder than arithmetic. Even patriots grow
despondent when taxes are too heavy. To expect families
of low and moderate income to surrender 50 percent or
more of earnings to the Internal Revenue Service is to
expect more of human nature in an acquisitive society

than on precedent human nature is prepared to yield. There is a second, equally conclusive argument against pay-as-you-go financing of protracted wars. Effective prosecution of these conflicts implies movement of millions of people from their usual occupations and present residences to new jobs located in unfamiliar communities hundreds or thousands of miles away. In totalitarian societies, governments may try to compel their subjects to endure these personal dislocations. In practice, even totalitarian systems supplement coercion by economic incentive. Democratic countries minimize coercion in favor of therapeutic blends of exhortation and appeals to individual interest. By far the least equivocal way to persuade people to fill war jobs is to pay them more. However, if most of the extra money is taken away, who would bother to come from afar for the pleasures of paying larger taxes?

In England and the United States, such assessments as these led public authorities to raise taxes as much as they dared and to borrow the remainder of what was needed to support the war machine. In this country, a few numbers summarize the impact of these decisions.

FEDERAL TAXES, EXPENDITURES,
DEFICITS, AND NATIONAL DEBT: 1939–1945 (in millions of dollars)

Year	Taxes	Expenditures	Deficit	National Debt
1939	$4,979	$8,841	$3,862	$40,440
1940	5,137	9,055	3,918	42,960
1941	7,096	13,255	6,159	48,961
1942	12,547	34,037	21,490	72,422
1943	21,948	79,368	57,420	136,696
1944	43,563	94,986	51,423	201,003
1945	44,362	98,303	53,941	258,682

Source: *Economic Report of the President,* January 1964.

Between 1939 and 1945, tax receipts multiplied tenfold for three reasons. The economy under pressure of war expanded so rapidly that even at 1939 prices and wages, the Treasury would have been a major beneficiary. Of course 1945 prices were considerably above 1939 prices, and the dollar totals for both income and tax liability were commensurately swollen. And tax rates were increased and steepened in progression in the interests of both revenue and social equity. For if a few were asked to sacrifice their lives, more to risk crippling injury, and millions to suffer in varying degree deprivations of freedom, income, and professional opportunity, then surely those who kept the home fires burning ought in justice to pay severe taxes. Congress found such reasoning compelling when in 1942 it imposed excess profits levies and raised the rates applicable to personal income. At war's beginning, only four million rather prosperous citizens filed income tax returns. By 1944, forty-two million were sharing in this fiscal rite of spring.

Even though after 1942 Congress raised taxes annually, deficits soared above $50 billion each year and stayed there. A mere $40 billion in 1939, the national debt was six times that sum by V-J Day in 1945.

Where did the money come from? Some flowed to the Treasury from the more or less voluntary purchases of war bonds out of military and civilian savings. Particularly in the armed services, the pressures to enroll in payroll-deduction bond-purchase schemes were severe enough to constitute an informal variant of compulsory saving.

The rest of the money for the war economy was created by the Federal Reserve System. In more primitive times, governments which urgently required cash simply printed it. A mark of sovereignty is traditionally regulation of the money supply. In our day, central bankers have devised more sophisticated modes of money creation. The process is neat. Needing money to pay its bills, the Treasury sells new bonds on attractively engraved paper to the Federal Reserve banks, this country's version of a central bank. The Federal Reserve pays for the bonds by increasing the Treasury's deposit account. On this account, even as you and I, the Treasury writes checks to pay its bills.

For their part, the suppliers and employees who get the Treasury checks deposit them in their own commercial banks. These banks—Chase Manhattan, First National City, and their smaller rivals—use their new deposits as the legal reserves against which they make new loans or renew old ones to businessmen of all varieties. As economists define money, the bulk of the stuff consists of rights to draw checks on these demand deposit accounts in commercial banks. The United States government, by selling securities issued by the Treasury (an instrument of government) to the Federal Reserve (another one), enlarges commercial bank deposits and the supply of money.

Moral: Responsible governments don't print money directly—they print bonds first.

However created, new money threatens price and wage stability. When wars are financed partly by debt (and money) creation, it is essential to supplement war finance by controls over incomes and prices. During World War II the Office of Price Administration, where, just graduated from Duke Law School, the young Richard Nixon briefly and unhappily worked, exercised detailed restraints upon the prices of practically everything bought and sold. Its companion agency, the War Labor Board, weathering the storms whipped up by John L. Lewis and his militant mine workers, managed to keep wages more or less in line with prices.

The effort would almost certainly have faltered if the country had been less united in a determination to defeat the Germans and the Japanese. Very likely, controls would have foundered under the sheer pressure of the masses of money that were floating about seeking a home if it had not been for the invention of a supplementary currency. Ration stamps for gasoline, meat, sugar, coffee, shoes, tires, and other scarce consumer goods amounted to the requirement that prospective customers bring to market two varieties of money, regular $5 and $10 bills and the correct number of ration stamps. Thus rationing was a device for bringing into approximate equality at controlled prices available supplies and allowable demand. Rationing was also an instrument of social justice, for in its absence the affluent in a thrice would have snapped up, at prices only they could afford, the goods in greatest demand and shortest supply.

No one old enough to recall the war years is likely to assert that this combination of taxes, bond drives, controls, and rationing worked smoothly and equitably. There were repetitive scandals. With admirable flexibility counterfeiters shifted from faking currency to faking ration stamps. More than one housewife bribed more than one butcher for first crack at first-cut beef. More than one shirt manufacturer evaded the spirit of price regulation by phasing out plain, white shirts in favor of fancier items with wider collars and wider profit margins. More than one union struck, war or no war.

All the same, wartime controls did work. Serious economic malfunction never impeded the war effort. Between 1940 and 1945 the cost of living edged upward less than 30 percent,* between 5 and 6 percent annually. Scarce as workers became in the last years of the war, wage rates rose in the same interval of time in real terms less than 20 percent, in dollar terms from $0.66 to $1.02 per hour in manufacturing.

---

*In 1940 the index stood at 48.8 (1957–1959=100). By 1945 the figure was 62.7. In 1949, *after* controls were removed (in 1946), the index soared to 83.

Wartime controls worked for two major reasons. The country was united behind a popular Chief Executive in pursuit of clear national objectives. And the controls were judged to deal rough justice to the major economic interests, at least most of the time. By war's end, American factories and farms were producing unprecedented masses of goods for civilians as well as the war machine. The scale and duration of the challenge were unprecedented. So also was the size of the achievement.

2.

It is human, not merely American, nature that once the war is over and the soldiers come marching home again, the heart turns to thoughts of red meat, new houses, shiny cars, and the other artifacts of consumer civilization. From the producers and merchandisers of these good things and their Madison Avenue agents comes the siren song of economic freedom. Only liberate us from rationing and price controls, run the lyrics, and we will swamp America with porterhouse and four-door sedans. By now weary of wartime austerity, the customers are the hucksters' natural allies. In the 1946 election, Republicans won control of Congress for the first time since the 1920s mostly on the cry of more meat and freer consumer markets. Soon afterward, World War II controls expired. Once the lid was off, the returning veterans and the celebrating civilians spent what they had reluctantly saved and sent prices sharply higher.

The post-Korean experience was similar. The consumer price index, which in 1950 was 83.8 percent of its 1957–1959 average, had five years later ascended to 93.3, and in 1960 stood at 103.1. The record testifies to the difficulties of controlling inflation once it has well and truly begun. For during the 1952 presidential campaign, Republicans had been particularly concerned about prices and especially certain that they knew what had to be done to improve their behavior: reduce federal spending.

In pursuit of fiscal austerity, the Eisenhower Administration started bravely enough. Assisted by the Korean peace dividend, the President in 1954, 1955, and 1956 pushed the level of federal expenditure down from 1953's $58 billion to $47.5, $45.3, and $45.7. Although appropriations edged upward after 1956, this was never an Administration of big spenders and always a group of true believers in a sound dollar. The search for this veritable White Whale led the Republicans to preside over three recessions, average unemployment in excess of 5 percent, and such low rates of economic growth that John Kennedy was able effectively to campaign on the promise of getting the country moving again. As ever in plutocracies, the gains of inflation flowed mostly to businessmen and speculators. The penalties of recession were inflicted primarily on the black, young, and female, groups which are particularly vulnerable to unemployment.

Although it is hard to be fair to Republicans, their economic policies during the 1950s did finally reduce the inflationary fever and transform business and consumer psychology. The experience left behind it a nagging question which has resurfaced in the 1970s with renewed urgency: Why is it so exceedingly difficult and socially so expensive to control inflation even in an Administration which gives this objective top priority and accepts as a price unemployment and lagging growth?

I propose to postpone temporarily consideration of the possible solution to the puzzle, in commemoration of a happy interlude, 1961–1965, during which it appeared that between them the economists and the politicians had finally evolved policies which successfully combined high employment, steady growth, and civilized price and wage behavior. Although it now appears that this Golden Age had a lot of good luck in it, there are lessons still to be derived.

Early in 1966 when Walter Heller, who as chairman of the Kennedy Council of Economic Advisers played a key role in designing policy and convincing the President of its efficacy, came to reflect on the implications of recent experience, he asserted that

Economics has come of age in the 1960s. Two presidents have recognized and drawn on modern economics as a source of national strength and Presidential power. Their willingness to use, for the first time, the full range of modern economic tools underlies the unbroken U.S. expansion since early 1961—an expansion that in its first five years created over seven million new jobs, doubled profits, increased the nation's real output by a third, and closed the $50-billion gap between actual and potential production that plagued the American economy in 1961.

Still more promisingly for future policy, a second gap was also closed:

Together with the gradual closing of that huge production gap has come—part as cause, part as consequence—a gradual, then rapid, narrowing of the intellectual gap between professional economists and men of affairs, between economic advisers and decision makers. The paralyzing grip of economic myth and false fears on policy has has been loosened, perhaps even broken.*

With pardonable, proprietorial pride, Walter Heller was celebrating John Kennedy's achievement in getting

*See his *New Dimensions of Political Economy* (New York: Harvard U. Press, 1966), p. 1.

the country moving again, as well as the circumstance, cheering to economists, that he had relied on the magic of modern economic theory. There really was something to brag about—for the moment. When the Democrats assumed office in 1961, the economy had already begun to recover from the third Republican recession, but it was a painfully gentle upward incline which like its 1958– 1959 predecessor might easily have ended well before full employment had been approximated. Concerned about this possibility, Mr. Kennedy in 1961 and 1962 nevertheless proceeded cautiously in the hope that small new expenditures on area development and manpower training, higher business investment stimulated by the new device of an investment tax credit, and expanded military and space programs would turn the trick.

They did not quite do so. Something more was needed, a major stimulus to the total demand for goods and services. It is the spending of businessmen, consumers, and government which creates jobs. Yet no American President had yet explicitly embraced the central proposition of Keynesian economics that recession was an ailment of deficient aggregate demand, a financial anemia which could best be relieved by the injection of generous quantities of green corpuscles.

Keynesians pointed to two alternative techniques of administration. One could, as John Kenneth Galbraith strenuously argued within Kennedy councils, simply spend more federal money on desirable public objectives, the familiar and long list which includes environmental restoration, public housing, delivery of health services, mass transit, aid to schools, and public jobs. Such had been the central theme of Galbraith's best-selling *The Affluent Society,* a polemic against the shame of public-sector poverty amid private-sector abundance.

However, as a matter of fiscal hydraulics, much the same effect could be anticipated from a tax cut, for one could count on grateful Americans to spend somewhere between 92 and 94 percent of any unexpected disposable income that came their way. Hence, if taxes were cut $10 or $11 billion, consumers would, after they got used to their new affluence, expand their purchases by $9½ billion or so. And better still, their expenditures would predictably enlarge the incomes of retailers and their clerks, wholesalers and their employees, and manufacturers and their operatives. This benign multiplier process would surely expand Gross National Product by several times the value of the original impetus.

Larger public spending promotes the public sector and lower taxes expand the private sector. To choose tax reduction instead of larger social spending is to make a choice of social priority, as well as to encourage taxpayer hopes of additional tax slashes and to threaten the Treasury's long-term capacity to finance social programs. President Kennedy appears to have followed the route of tax reduction out of native conservatism as well as out of the political judgment that Congress just might grant $10–$11 billion in tax benefits to the voters but would certainly not embark on social spending anywhere close to the scale required to shove the economy onto a convincing full-employment growth path.

In the aftermath of President Nixon's enrollment as a Keynesian, it is easy to discount the political courage required in 1962 of a President to deliberately run a large budget deficit during a period of recovery in the interests of still faster economic expansion. Although in point of fact only three of the Eisenhower budgets had been balanced, President Eisenhower and his impeccably reactionary Secretaries of the Treasury George Humphrey and Robert Anderson had never ceased to sing the virtues of budget balance and deplore its elusiveness. There was something attractive about a young President who was candid enough to confide in a Yale commencement audience (in June 1962) the news that balanced budgets were merely technical tools, not articles of political theology. As Mr. Kennedy put his heterodoxy: "The myth persists that federal deficits create inflation and budget surpluses prevent it." Against this myth, the President opposed recent history: ". . . sizable budget surpluses after the war did not prevent inflation and persistent deficits for the last several years have not upset our basic price stability." Mr. Kennedy advised his auditors and other sensible Americans to draw the evident moral: "Obviously deficits are sometimes dangerous and so are surpluses. But honest assessment plainly requires a more sophisticated view than the old and automatic cliché that deficits automatically bring inflation."

Yale is one thing and the case-hardened veterans of the congressional wars another. Still, it was arguments like these that the White House deployed against the congressional elders who controlled the House Ways and Means and the Senate Finance committees, at the time Wilbur Mills and the late Walter George. Just before the Dallas assassination, nearly a year after Mr. Kennedy had addressed his tax-reduction proposal to Congress, its legislative fate was still in some doubt. But in February 1964, Congress finally gave its approval.

Remarkable to recall, healthy reductions in personal and corporate taxes ($10–$11 billion worth) had almost precisely the impact on growth and employment which the partisans of the policy predicted. Unemployment sagged toward the 4 percent interim target which had been enunciated by the Council of Economic Advisers, the gap between potential and actual Gross National Product pleasingly narrowed, and the 2½ multiplier estimated by the Council of Economic Advisers approximated in real life this hoped-for value.

Almost best of all, prices behaved, in part because the economy was operating still at less than full capacity, also because inflationary expectations had not yet been aroused, and finally because the Council of Economic Advisers had stated and occasionally enforced a set of more or less voluntary wage and price guidelines which imposed moderate restraints upon powerful corporations and strong trade unions.

In the 1960s the atmosphere was transformed from the gray sobriety of the Eisenhower days to a New Economics euphoria. Only a year or so earlier, Treasury Secretary Humphrey had raised his voice against the heresy that the country could "spend ourselves rich." Theodore White, the chronicler of presidential campaigns, had reported that "Scores of Congressmen, and Senators, Democrats and Republicans, are viscerally terrified that the unbalanced Budget will destroy the dollar, the life savings, insurance policies and civilized life of Americans all together."

By the time Congress had completed its historic deliberations, the highly respectable magazine *Business Week* was prepared to call the tax cut "the triumph of an idea," and to boast of the important role played in its passage by Henry Ford II's Business Committee for Tax Reduction. The flexible Wilbur Mills, who had begun with the view that "The function of taxation is to raise revenue. . . . I do not go along with economists who think of taxation primarily as an instrument for manipulating the economy," in the end released the bill from his committee and himself managed its passage through the House of Representatives.

For a moment or two, politicians, businessmen, business journals, and economists were united behind the principle that the national budget really was an appropriate "instrument for manipulating the economy." In that Cambridge spring, Dr. Heller dwelled with the pride of a victorious warrior after the battle was over. He and the other New Frontier–Great Society economists dared hope that they had discovered the secret of steady, noninflationary growth—without recession.

Economic détente, like the Great Society which chronologically escorted it, was short-lived. What blighted inflation-free growth and social reform was the tragedy of Vietnam. War and inflation are particularly compatible under the peculiar circumstances which surrounded mounting American commitments to a distant civil conflict. Although, as twentieth-century American wars go, Vietnam was comparatively small, there were several reasons why its inflationary impact was bound to be severe. It commenced, unlike World War II, in the train of an expansion which had pushed the economy perilously close to capacity operation. Since the conflict was undeclared, full of ambiguities which limited popular appeal, and escalated by discreet stages, it never was politically possible to whip up the patriotic fervor which smoothed the path of earlier war presidents.

There was a special ingredient in this high policy stew. Lyndon Johnson, whose durable political hero was the Roosevelt of the New Deal, had pushed and shoved a huge assortment of social legislation through a balky Congress. The Great Society had plausible title as the first major social-reform thrust since the first term of Franklin Roosevelt. What would become of the "unconditional" War on Poverty, Head Start, Title I grants to poor school districts, Medicare, Medicaid, regional health centers, job corps camps, VISTA, rent supplements, and the other children of the Great Society, when their Texas white father had to ask Congress for the tax increases, rationing, and controls which had been staples of previous war economies? The precedent was grim and clear. After Pearl Harbor, Franklin Roosevelt announced that henceforth he was Doctor Win-the-War. Dr. New Deal, averred the Chief Executive, was retired for the duration. Lyndon Johnson had genuine reason to fear that the price of candor on the topic of Vietnam was wholesale slaughter of his infant social programs.

The war and the Great Society both grew in expense. Federal spending joined business investment and lavish consumer buying as expansions of aggregate demand and pressures upon price stability. At the very latest, a major tax rise was needed in early 1966—or a withdrawal from Vietnam. The moment came and passed. Willfully or otherwise, the Pentagon underestimated by $10 billion the likely cost of another year of Asiatic war. Though uneasy and unhappy, the Council of Economic Advisers, headed by Michigan's Gardner Ackley, nevertheless refrained from public recommendation of tax increase in the January 1966 *Economic Report of the President.* By the time, early in 1967, that Mr. Johnson reluctantly asked Congress to enact a surcharge on personal and corporate income, inflation had taken off, expectations of even more inflation pushed prices, wages, and interest rates still higher, and Congress aggravated unease by taking over fifteen months to complete its action on the surcharge.

In economic lingo, this was a classic demand-pull inflation. More dollars were being paid out in income by employers, public and private, than could be matched (without raising prices) by the producers of raw materials, machines, and consumer goods. As markets registered the pressures of eager buyers upon them, prices stirred and leaped, unemployment fell below 3.5 percent, less than it had been in any month since Korean War days, and the boom grew wilder as expectations of further inflation spread.

In January 1969 Vietnam, which had elected Richard Nixon, presented him as President with a distorted economy. Although unemployment was pleasingly low, inflation was distressingly high. The policy dilemma was acute. Mr. Nixon was ruefully aware of his party's reputation for tenderness to businessmen and hard-heartedness to the unemployed. In *My Six Crises,* he had recalled with pain how he had lost the 1960 contest because unemployment rose during an election year and the Administration which he served as Vice-President refused to take vigorous action against it. It wouldn't take a great deal to remind the middle-aged survivors of the Great Depression of Herbert Hoover and possibly send their children with unwonted alacrity to historical accounts of the 1930s. For that matter, even the young could recall the bad job market of the Eisenhower 1950s. If the suspicion hardened into conviction that Republicans brought bad times with them, not many Republicans would in the future make it to the White House.

Such were the politics of the condition. However, conventional economic wisdom held that checking inflation required both monetary and fiscal maneuvers of dispiriting varieties. When the Federal Reserve restricts monetary growth, interest rates rise for home buyers, local governments, school districts, farmers, and local merchants. Families who bought autos on the never-never, which is to say most families, faced larger monthly installments. The news was equally glum fiscally. The experts advised higher taxes or lower federal spending. The former policy carried in its train smaller take-home pay, diminished consumer purchases, shrinking business profits, blighted investment prospects, and fewer jobs. Pruning the budget was not necessarily less painful. Firing bureaucrats for the greater good is slender comfort for the human sacrifices. If the elderly, sick, unemployed, and poor are granted fewer benefits, they will necessarily retaliate by spending less. This time the multiplier impact is downward. A $10 billion tax hike or expenditure slash multiplies itself several times over as in successive rounds new groups of merchants, wholesalers, processors, and wage earners grapple with the consequences of fewer sales and smaller weekly earnings.

The President and his advisers naturally wondered whether inflation could be squeezed out of the system so gradually that the impact upon unemployment and economic growth would be so nearly imperceptible as scarcely to merit the title of recession. To ask the question is almost to mandate an affirmative answer. Hence the initial Administration game plan was "gradualism." The most skilled practitioners of the black political arts want their cake and want to eat it too. So it occurred that in 1969 and 1970 the Federal Reserve, under the direction initially of William McChesney Martin and then of the President's old friend and adviser Dr. Arthur F. Burns (the only economist ever to occupy the position of Federal Reserve chairman), clamped down on the growth of money and credit. The President complemented monetary action by seeking to restrain federal spending and initiating troop withdrawals from Indochina.

Although White House spokesmen put a resolutely cheerful face on the progress of gradualism,* it was manifest, at least to men and women scrambling for scarce jobs, small businessmen struggling to avert bankruptcy, and economists not in the employ of the Administration, that the game plan was faltering. Not that it had no impact. It did generate a slowdown, just as the seers had advised. Stabilization of military outlays and reduction by a half of the 1968 enlargement of the money supply had reduced real economic growth from 4.7 percent in 1968 to 2.3 percent in 1969. By early 1970, output was actually declining and a new, though fortunately mild, recession was in progress.

Such was the cost of gradualism. The product, alas, was distressingly slight. The Consumer Price Index fluctuated around a 6 percent rate of increase in 1969 and

---

*Of Dr. Harold Passer, one of these spokesmen, it was said that he had never encountered a statistic that he didn't love.

actually rose to 6½ percent early in 1970. Thereafter, with month-to-month fluctuations, the index slid downward to 5 percent in midyear and 4 percent by year's end. Administration loyalists might have taken heart even from this glacial response to their efforts, save for the unemployment statistics which accompanied the price reports. Unemployment which averaged nearly 5 percent in 1970 increased to an average of nearly 6 percent in the following year. In the 1970 election the poor Republican showing sharply warned the President that if the economy did not soon display improvement, he was likely to be retired from the White House in 1972 and his party labeled as people who knew better how to lose their constituents' jobs than to lower the prices they had to pay for the necessities and comforts of life. Although the President had promised to do better, his first two years in office more nearly resembled Eisenhower's recessions than Kennedy's prosperity. The Administration's plan to scotch the snake of inflation without unleashing the dragon of recession proved as secret as the famous blueprint for ending the Vietnam war.

Mr. Nixon was not the President to misinterpret the political storm signals. At the start of 1971 he casually announced that in economic policy he was now a Keynesian, a revelation that set veteran Keynesians to wondering whether the doctrine was now obsolete. The same politician who in 1969 had promised to balance the federal budget so that middle Americans might better balance their family budgets now explained that what he really meant was the full-employment budget. The new rule and target were to match federal spending and Treasury tax receipts only when full recovery and full employment adequately raised the receipts from levies on corporate and personal income. Until that day of glory, the President was proud of his actual deficits in less-than-full-employment budgets. Actually, these were the largest peacetime deficits in American history.

And even before the President announced his conversion, the Federal Reserve had begun to reinflate the money supply. The 1971 increase was to be 6.2 percent, up from 1970's 5.4 percent and 1969's mere 3.1 percent. More money promised lower interest rates for installment buyers, prospective home owners, local governments, and small businessmen. Manifestly, even though inflation had not been exorcised, the President was perforce at length more concerned about unemployment, possibly because 6 percent rates of joblessness threatened the prosperity not merely of blacks, Chicanos, and urbanites who either voted wrong or not at all, but also of aerospace engineers, advertising executives, and other real (Republican) people. At such juncture of events, unemployment presents itself as a political, not a trivial human problem.

Yet, despite his public statements which professed a sharp turn in economic policy, the President had done little more than publicly describe existing budgetary relationships and openly endorse the monetary ease independently prescribed by the Federal Reserve. Under the circumstances it was not especially startling that nothing spectacular occurred. Investors, euphoric over the President's words, did not double capital-spending plans. Consumers failed to celebrate in the supermarkets and showrooms. Recovery from the 1969–1970 recession proceeded, albeit very slowly, and unemployment continued to rise, as it often does at the very start of mild recoveries. In the first half of 1971 the inflation rate continued to hover around 4 percent.

Congressional Democrats and Great Society economists, and also a growing band of Republicans worried about their political prospects and businessmen oppressed by unsatisfactory profit margins, began to clamor for price and wage controls, as well as more fiscal stimulation. At first Mr. Nixon resisted these demands. In June he convened a Camp David conference, attended by his most important economic counselors—George P. Shultz (then director of the Office of Management and Budget), John B. Connally (still a Democrat but also Secretary of the Treasury), Dr. Herbert Stein (then a member and subsequently chairman of the Council of Economic Advisers), Dr. Paul W. McCracken (then CEA chairman), and, naturally, Dr. Arthur F. Burns.

In the light of rapidly unfolding events, the Camp David conclave had certain comic consequences. Out of it emerged Dr. Shultz with the assurance that the game plan was working, just be patient, and the right watchword was "Steady as you go." Secretary Connally told the world in bold Texas language that the Administration had no plan to intervene directly in wages and prices and thus abridge economic liberty. In July the unlucky Dr. McCracken wrote a sharp article in the Washington *Post,* specifically attacking J. K. Galbraith, and arguing that controls, always an inferior policy, were particularly ill advised at the present moment because most of the inflation had occurred either in competitive industries or in medical and other services, rather than in the concentrated industries identified by Galbraith as important culprits.

The public clamor continued and if peace with honor was not yet at hand, the 1972 election indisputably became ever more imminent. Business periodicals like *Business Week* called for controls. The AFL-CIO's George Meany reasserted his support for "equitable" restraints over wages, other incomes, and prices. In politics as in other aspects of life, what counts is appearances. These were against an Administration which, fairly or not, was perceived to be as inactive in its Keynesian phase as earlier it had been in its Friedmanite experiments with the money supply.*

---

*Professor Milton Friedman, who will reappear from time to time in this

On many an occasion President Nixon had expressed his detestation of controls and recalled with abhorrence his spell of service in the Office of Price Administration. August 15, 1971, was the day on which these statements became inoperative.* Mr. Nixon had plans to visit Peking and Moscow. In spirit he now reached out to Cambridge, Massachusetts, and recruited John Kenneth Galbraith. Not, of course, that the dreadful name was ever uttered. Still, it was a matter of public record that Dr. Galbraith was one of the few economists of reputation who in season and out had argued for the necessity of permanent wage and price controls focused on the numerous industries where giant corporations exercised decisive influence over market prices. On this enchanted Sunday evening the President went even further than his unadmitted guide had counseled. He imposed a total freeze on incomes and prices for ninety days and promised a detailed set of regulations after the freeze. For good measure, he placed a 10 percent tariff surcharge on imports, suspended gold.sales, revived the investment tax credit (retitled Job Development Credits), reduced auto excise taxes, and proposed lightening personal income-tax levies.

It was as though the President, stung into action by political necessity, had decided to bewilder the universe by accepting simultaneously all or most of his critics' recommendations: import surcharges for the protectionists, severing of the link between gold and the dollar for followers of Milton Friedman, who had persistently advocated freely floating currencies, fiscal stimulation

chronicle, holds to the faith that the way to control inflation is to permit the money supply to expand at a steady rate consistent with the growth of real output.

*The usage is of course that made famous by Press Secretary Ronald Ziegler in recanting the cloud of denials of Watergate malfeasance which he had uttered on behalf of the President.

through investment tax credits and other tax benefits for the Keynesians, and controls for the Galbraithians and their allies in the business and labor community. No wonder, as one commentator amiably put it, that Administration policies struck him as "the most comprehensive economics in the history of the world," spacious enough to house under the White House roof "Friedmanism and Keynesianism, laissez faire and price controls, mercantilism and free trade, the ideologies of free enterprise and social responsibilities."*

Phase I, as this policy collage was immediately termed, was the high point of the President's first-term economic policy. Although well-publicized squabbles with George Meany over the shape of post-freeze controls disturbed the general harmony, relief was general that, however belatedly, the Administration was acting in the interests of average Americans afflicted with average worries about rising prices and job security.

Phase II controls, which began in November, featured one of those bureaucratic inventions of which Republican regimes seem particularly fond. There was a seven-man Price Commission, presided over by a business-school dean, C. Jackson Grayson, who displayed considerable public relations talent. The commission mandated for the large corporations' prenotification of price increases, detailed justification for their necessity, and profit margins no larger than those of the best two of the three preceeding years. Merchants were instructed to post lists of base-period prices and keep records of any changes in them that they made.

Complementing the Price Commission was a Pay Board, headed by an elderly judge innocent of previous experience in labor-management relations, and initially

*The quoted words are those of the *New York Times'* Leonard Silk. See his *Nixonomics* (New York: Praeger, 1972), p. 205.

composed of labor, public, and business members. It set a 5.5 percent standard for wage and salary increases which, as time passed, was frequently bent and ingeniously interpreted but never quite destroyed as a check on union demands and the size of ultimate contract settlements. Supervising both agencies and determining their jurisdiction was a Cost of Living Council directly responsible to the President. It was headed by Donald Rumsfeld, a former congressman and director of the Office of Economic Opportunity.

Although trade-union grumbling was loud and most of the labor representatives early walked off the Pay Board, Phase II controls worked well enough so that as 1972 drew to a close, most observers of the economy, including Dr. Burns, assumed and advised their continuance into 1973. It was not to be. Indulging his penchant for surprises and reversals of form, the President on January 11 abruptly terminated Phase II and replaced it with a far vaguer set of Phase III standards.

Under Phase III it was unclear whether the 5.5 percent wage guideline remained in force. John D. Ehrlichman, then still Mr. Nixon's chief domestic adviser, implied that it did not. Ronald Ziegler suggested that Mr. Ehrlichman had misspoken. George Meany sounded as though repeal of the guideline had been part of what the President had promised him in return for his benevolent neutrality during the presidential race. On the price side, there was rather more clarity. The major corporations no longer needed Price Commission approval before they lifted prices. For one thing, there no longer was to be a Price Commission to bother them. The President had at a stroke eliminated it and the Pay Board as well.

One can only speculate about the reasons for the President's actions. One possibility was that the controls were beginning to hurt. As the boom gathered momentum, corporations found themselves in a position to make considerably larger profits than the Phase II limitations permitted. Proud to preside over a pro-business government, Mr. Nixon had ample reason to be grateful to the large corporations which had heavily contributed to his electoral landslide. He also had his debts to the Meany wing of the labor movement.

Ideology probably supplemented political obligation. In his official family the economists were devoted free marketeers, able in the best Chicago tradition to perceive competition where it was invisible to others.* Drs. Shultz and Stein had reluctantly and loyally designed and administered Phase I and Phase II, but they longed to shed controls at the earliest opportunity. In fairness to these gentlemen and their colleagues, outside economists misjudged the state of the economy almost as severely. Walter Heller, Gardner Ackley, and Arthur Okun, the three Kennedy-Johnson CEA chairmen, supported the President's bold initiative. On January 13, 1973, the *New York Times* headlined their response: "3 DEMOCRATIC ECONOMISTS BACK PHASE 3 STRUCTURE AND PRINCIPLES." The *Times* subhead noted that "Heller, Ackley and Okun Are Joined by Dr. Burns, Who Voices Full Support."

Practically nobody else applauded. The stock market plummeted and the Dow-Jones index daily registered the fears of investors that renewed inflation could lead to only one result: another savage credit squeeze and a new recession. Major corporations interpreted Phase III as full of sound and fury, signifying nothing. They flocked to post new and higher prices. A new run on the dollar, led by American multinational firms, the major

---

*Conventional economists prefer competition to monopoly. The Chicago School, currently led by Milton Friedman, is not only passionate about this preference but prone to minimize the extent of monopoly and market power in the United States.

international banks, and the oil sheiks of the Middle East, in short order compelled Washington to devalue the dollar for the second time in fourteen months. Food prices soared higher and higher. A nationwide meat boycott angered farmers, and while it relieved the feelings of the meat-eating public, it did nothing to lower the price of hamburger, let alone steak. Rich from their booming export sales, the Japanese were widely suspected of collaring the supply of the best American beef. Ever eager to see the silver lining, an Administration spokesman pointed out that the Japanese buying policy had the beneficial effect of increasing the availability of the cheaper cuts which they had used to buy when they were poorer.

Food prices are subject to the impact of bad weather, international politics, and domestic crop limitations. What was still more ominous was the escalation of nonfood prices. Industrial materials began to climb in price at annual rates over 12 percent. An impending energy crisis persuaded the President to postpone application of the standards of the Clean Air Act.

No one in his right mind could have argued in the spring of 1973 that inflation was under control. All that two and a half years of recovery from the 1969–1970 recession had done for jobs was to reduce unemployment from 6 to 5 percent. By the middle of 1973, "The big debate among economists is whether 1974 will witness a recession or not."* The consolation was slim that a narrow majority thought that expansion would continue, though at a slower pace. Societies that conduct their affairs on hope and credit are vulnerable to even mild attempts by monetary authorities to restrict money and credit and shove interest rates upward. Investors could scarcely help but recall that the "mild" 1969–1970

*See *Business Week* (May 26, 1973), p. 19.

recession had doubled unemployment, starting from December 1969's 3.3 percent rate. Recession in 1974, starting from 5 percent unemployment threatened 10 percent general rates of unemployment and far higher joblessness among youths, blacks, Chicanos, and women.*

---

*For reasons that will subsequently emerge, the official unemployment figures drastically understate the extent of the problem. A multiplier of two is a realistic corrective.

II.
The Causes

After a cycle of Milton Friedman, John Maynard Keynes, and John Kenneth Galbraith, here was a sufficiently depressing condition of affairs. Although the country was not unhappily mired in a Hoover-style depression in 1973, neither had the politicians and the economists between them learned how to reconcile full employment and price stability.

An elderly citizen contemplating retirement might have wondered about the extent of economic enlightenment in his lifetime. A person born in 1908 and retiring in 1973 no doubt found his first job during the prosperity of the 1920s, briefly celebrated as a "permanent plateau of prosperity." Unless his luck was good, he lost that job during the 1930s when the Great Depression threw out of employment more than a quarter of the labor force and a worker counted himself fortunate to wangle a place on the WPA rolls. Although a measure of recovery occurred during the first Roosevelt Administration, a sharp new recession dashed hope in 1937 and 1938. On the very eve of Pearl Harbor, in December 1941, unemployment was still a sickening 14 percent and economists were gravely writing of the danger of permanent stagnation in the American economy.*

Our prospective pensioner, thirty-three years old when his country entered World War II, might have served in the armed forces as a volunteer or draftee. More probably, he found a job in the booming war plants, where his earnings (including overtime) almost surely exceeded by a good deal the wages of his previous working life. Postwar reconversion could readily have entailed a spell of unemployment, followed by the Korean War boom, the sluggish economy of the 1950s, the continued slow growth of the early 1960s, that brief, happy interlude in the mid-1960s when high employment and low prices peacefully coexisted, and then the inflationary alarums of the Vietnam era.

White or black, our senior citizen was almost surely living better at the close than at the start of his career in the labor market, although the income of the black was on the odds lower and his experience of unemployment more extensive than that of his white colleagues. This said, it is equally true that except for four or five years when he began work as a youth and a similar period at the end of his productive years, our sixty-five-year-old lived through years in which either unemployment, inflation, wartime controls and shortages, or a combination among these conditions darkened his hopes and threatened his job and income.

To repeat with emphasis, 1973 was better than 1933. Politicians and even economists do learn from experience. Depression, which in 1933 was accepted by con-

---

*In 1938 the dean of American Keynesians, Harvard's Alvin Hansen, delivered as his American Economic Association presidential address an analysis of the reasons why economic growth in the United States was likely to be slow. The frontier was closed. Population growth had diminished. Because of monopoly, among other causes, invention was likely to become less important as a source of new investment.

servatives as an act of God or punishment for financial excess and interpreted by the learned as necessary wage-price readjustments to altered market conditions, was viewed in the later year as a condition amenable to the enlightened policies of concerned political leaders. In our day, no President or prime minister can anticipate political survival in the presence of really severe unemployment for any protracted period.

This is a test which the Nixon Administration, as conservative in its inclinations as any American government since William Howard Taft, passed when in early 1971 it turned Keynesian and later in the same year interventionist. Six percent unemployment turns the most devoted of free-market ideologues into an economic tinkerer —when he happens to be a President eligible for re-election. In the 1930s a mere 6 percent unemployment figure would have appeared something to celebrate, by no means a signal for renewed fiscal stimulation and monetary ease.

Very sensibly the community expects governments to control unemployment. This is the enduring legacy of John Maynard Keynes, whose great *General Theory of Employment, Interest and Money* (1936) converted economists and then politicians to the proposition that depressions were neither theological judgments, essential readjustments, nor uncontrollable accidents. Ever so simply, they were the consequence of failure by the spenders— investors, consumers, and government, to buy enough goods and services to justify the number of jobs which corresponded to full employment.

In principle, the remedy was as simple as the diagnosis. Governments should spend more (without taxing more) or, in the alternative, help consumers and investors to spend more. It didn't much matter during a serious depression what government spent money on. As Keynes phrased it, in a bravura passage:

If the Treasury were to fill old bottles with bank-notes, bury them at suitable depths in disused coal-mines which are then filled up to the surface with town rubbish, and leave it to private enterprise on well-tried principles of *laissez-faire* to dig the notes up again . . . there need be no more unemployment and, with the help of the repercussions, the real income of the community, and its capital wealth also, would probably become a good deal greater than it actually is. It would indeed be more sensible to build houses and the like; but if there are political and practical difficulties in the way of this, the above would be better than nothing.*

Even the most original thinkers are prisoners of their own experience. During the 1920s, Keynes came increasingly to worry about unemployment and decreasingly about inflation, in part because the social costs of the first were more severe than those of the second. The 1930s, when inflation was a hypothetical menace and unemployment a pressing horror, intensified his emphasis. Accordingly, in his masterwork Keynes devoted little attention to inflation. Rather optimistically, as later events demonstrated, he assumed that it would become a problem only after his England or the United States had reached the neighborhood of full employment.

In the present essay, the moment has come to ask what went wrong. Why is it so difficult in advanced economies, here and abroad, to combine satisfactory patterns of prices and employment? Why have governments of assorted political colorations in Scandinavia, England, France, Japan, and the United States been obliged to intervene in the detailed decisions of sellers and unions —often against the proclaimed principles of the responsible officials?

Why, in a word, is contemporary inflation intractable?

*See *The General Theory of Employment, Interest and Money* (New York: Harcourt, Brace, 1936), p. 129.

2.

Until the 1950s, economists recognized only one kind of inflation, that which was caused by excess demand. Sometimes, but far from invariably, the immediate culprit was government and the occasion was war or its immediate aftermath. For when in spells of full employment (as in wartime) governments spend more than they collect in taxes and create new money to pay their remaining bills, the new money quickly translates into a demand for food, shelter, clothing, luxuries, and entertainment. Any economy running at full blast cannot readily expand the supply of these items. Hence the customers take to bidding against one another for what is available, retailers cross out old prices and happily substitute higher new ones, and at each stage of the productive and distributive process, shortages multiply and prices ascend.

During classic demand-pull inflation, wages rise *pari passu* with prices. Unorganized workers bargain individually with employers, easily extracting wage improvements because labor is scarce and their higher pay can readily be passed on in higher prices. As union contracts expire, new ones are negotiated, embodying large increases and, frequently, cost-of-living escalator clauses as protection against inflation during the life of the contract. As usual, higher labor costs stimulate higher prices, and each rise in the cost of living is the occasion for enlarged wage demands. The familiar price-wage spiral turns upward at ever steeper angles.

The original impetus can as readily arise from businessmen or consumers as from extravagant governments. The same sequence enacts itself when corporations embark on investment sprees (at moments of full employment), borrow money to finance their purchases, and persuade the Federal Reserve to expand commercial bank reserves by amounts large enough to justify the new investment loans. Or, if consumers take it into their heads to save less and spend more, dip into their savings accounts, and enlarge their mortgage and installment debts, they too can set off a demand inflation, on the usual condition that the monetary authorities cooperate, as usually they do, by expanding the supply of money and credit.

Even in our day, inflation usually begins as a demand phenomenon. In the middle of 1965, when our current inflation began, the economy was close to full employment of people and resources. It was in the middle of the fifth year of an economic expansion which began just before the inauguration of John Kennedy. Remarkably, in spite of a few signs of impending pressure on price stability, the consumer price index was still impressively steady and the voluntary wage-price guidelines preserved their credibility as deterrents to excessive price and wage demands.

Upon this reasonably stable situation of sustainable economic growth, President Johnson's Vietnam escalation imposed the strains already noted. Vietnam shattered a fragile harmony of interest among government, labor, and business. In 1964 and 1965, prosperity was raising wages and profits and swelling Treasury receipts. Out of this détente came the combination of tax reduction and social innovation which defined the Great Society.

The troops and the defense workers which Vietnam required drained manpower from civilian production. With the manpower went potential civilian output. The incomes which were generated in the war plants and in the armed services could not be spent on the planes, tanks, helicopters, uniforms, PX supplies, and Vietnam bomb craters that workers and airmen cooperated to produce and use. Defense-generated incomes simply added themselves to other incomes in the competition for civilian goods.

Because it was not until 1968 that Congress and the White House accepted the necessity of higher taxes to drain off this excess demand, inflationary expectations fed upon political inactivity. Unions, anticipating inflation, bargain for contracts which will compensate them for losses of real income imposed by an inflation that has already taken place and protect them against the inflation that is yet to come. Corporate employers, who at less inflationary moments resist far smaller union demands, now grant them out of fear that refusal will result in strikes that rob corporations of profitable sales, and out of anticipation that whatever is given unions can be passed on to consumers with profit sweeteners added to taste. Interest rates rise, not only because everybody is eager to borrow valuable dollars and pay back depreciated currency, but because banks and other lenders, aware of the same probabilities, raise interest rates as a hedge against the declining value of money.

This game of catch-up has no pleasant end. When the music halts, the losers' cries of anguish are heartfelt. Unions on the verge of new contracts sheltering them against the price blasts, companies at the point of posting higher price schedules reflecting their own swelling costs, and public employees about to extract from Congress and legislatures gains which will repair the erosions of inflation in civil service scales—all these and others will shout foul.

Traditionally the inflationary music is halted by monetary action taken by central-banking authorities. Although political governments exercise varying degrees of control over their central bankers, the central bankers themselves invariably detest inflation. Given the opportunity, central banks dampen inflation in ways which simultaneously appease the financial Calvinism latent in the central-banking soul and impose substantial losses if not actual disasters upon vulnerable borrowers—no doubt for the strengthening of their character.

When the Federal Reserve makes commercial-bank borrowing more expensive or even rations the credit it is willing to extend to member banks, then Chase Manhattan and First National City, as well as the financial minnows who swim in their wake, react in two ways: they happily charge their own customers higher interest and they diminish lending to their riskier customers. By preference, big banks deal with big borrowers. When General Motors deigns to borrow, it confers a regal favor upon the lender. When a small merchant petitions for credit to carry his inventories or finance his spring line, it is of course the loan officer of his bank who confers a favor. It ought to surprise no one that in a credit squeeze those who suffer least, if at all, are large corporations who borrow large amounts on a steady, long-term basis.

Nor is the identity of the individuals and institutions most afflicted any secret. In addition to small businessmen, the usual list runs to family farmers, school districts, local governments, and state authorities. A credit shortage implies fewer classrooms, sewage disposal plants, hospital beds, and other public facilities. The market mechanism is simple and deadly. A general rise in interest rates forces down the price of existing municipal and state bonds until, at reduced prices, the bonds yield the prevailing market return. A school or sewage district which tries to sell new bonds for additional facilities is compelled to promise much higher returns to purchasers, equivalent to the yields on existing securities, and raise property taxes by larger amounts to service the new debt.

If the central bankers maintain pressure long enough,

even giant borrowers begin to feel the pinch. Business is notoriously conducted on credit. A protracted credit squeeze causes retailers to delay payment of their bills. Their wholesalers stall manufacturers, who in turn reim- burse their own suppliers as late as they dare. The weaker brethren falter and fail. Invariably some nasty surprises astound the financial community. A Penn Central suddenly collapses. Peculiar events occur in the stock market. The stock of Four Seasons Nursing Homes plummets from 91 to zero and that of National Student Marketing from 36 to 1½. Can you lose money on kids and geriatric cases? Yes.

Only recently touted as the era's managerial miracle, conglomerates unexpectedly reveal the falling profits and actual losses which the stock-market boom and the imagination of their accountants had contrived to conceal. Tight money sends everybody frantically scurrying about and uncovers embarrassing quantities of fraud and coveys of quondam financial wizards. Hopes of sudden riches are dashed, small stock-market investors liquidate their holdings, bulls retreat, and bears dominate the stock exchanges. Even soundly managed enterprises encounter difficulty in raising new money in a sour market. Investment flags and consumers, saddened by the disappearance of their paper profits, curtail expenditure on vacations, expensive cars, and new appliances. It becomes quite apparent that the boom is an appallingly rickety structure, subject to the buffeting of disappointed hope and revelations of spreading fraud.

This is to say that demand-pull inflation usually ends as it did in 1969 and 1970 on the dying fall of recession, financial scandal, and major bankruptcy. During the 1950s, the three Eisenhower recessions were deliberate anti-inflationary acts of policy. Since 1945 England has under Labour and Conservative leaders endured stop-go episodes of alternatively tight and loose credit which have been factors in the unsatisfactory English economic record.

Of recession as a remedy for inflation, more will shortly be said. Here two propositions deserve emphasis. Recession is, to reiterate emphatically, a slow therapy. In two years all that the Nixon invocation of it achieved was slight moderation in the pace of price ascent at the price of considerable lost output and a doubled incidence of unemployment. Before his initial policy succeeded, the exigencies of the political calendar compelled the President to abandon it. The impact upon the British economy has been more severe and is likely to be more lasting. England, which a generation ago enjoyed the highest standard of living in western Europe, has in the 1970s fallen behind Sweden, Switzerland, France, and West Germany. If present trends continue, Japan and Italy will soon overtake England as well.

In 1973 it is apparent that the British have been done in by their characteristic virtues—extraordinary political discipline and high financial responsibility—for both major parties behaved more "responsibly" in the face of inflation and an adverse balance of international payments than parliamentary parties elsewhere or American Democrats and Republicans. On each occasion a boom loomed, prices and trading deficits increased, and whoever happened to be prime minister—Macmillan, Home, Wilson, or Heath, promptly slammed on the monetary and fiscal brakes. The rewards of financial virtue are slow growth, high unemployment, lagging improvements in the conditions of everyday living, and—the applause of central bankers. It scarcely seems an adequate reward.

As deliberate recession is usually arranged, the second judgment to be made of it is that it is outrageously unfair. It has already been noted that the burden of higher interest rates for the most part is borne by individuals and business enterprises, as well as public agencies, who are last in the borrowing queue. Efforts to restrain inflation seem somehow to stimulate limitations of Medicare benefits, reductions of welfare stipends, increases in the average size of public-school classes, and other exercises in deliberate meanness.

The unemployment generated by recession afflicts with special savagery blacks and other minorities whose seniority is shortest and formal credentials sketchiest. Thus, between 1953 and 1960 the ratio of black to white income fell from 57 to 51 percent, primarily because of black vulnerability to early layoffs. During the 1960s this ratio again rose, primarily because labor was in short supply, employers reduced credentials barriers, auto companies experimented with hiring of hard-core and high-risk men and women who sometimes sported extensive prison and arrest records, and civil rights statutes opened some doors that traditionally had been closed to blacks.

As the English economist Alfred Marshall wisely recommended, it is prudent to rely more heavily on the stronger rather than the higher human motives. It follows that altruism is a fragile tool in a genuine assault upon racial discrimination and its associated poverty and idleness. By exuberant contrast, a healthy boom and its attendant scarcities of workers are wonderful stimuli to recruitment into the labor force of all sorts of individuals who otherwise might not have been granted even a job interview. A 1965 study by the Office of Economic Opportunity concluded that a decline in general unemployment from 5.4 to 3.5 percent was likely to create 1,-042,000 new full-time jobs for poor workers and raise 1,811,000 individuals above the poverty line.

Just as recession encourages national meanness, prosperity promotes social generosity. It is worth recalling that Great Society programs were enacted and funded at a time of rapid growth, considerable social optimism, and for the prosperous, some soothing syrup in the guise of tax reduction. The fragile ties between white and black, union and nonunion worker, poor and prosperous are loosened by adversity. Unions are too obsessed with the preservation of their members' jobs to open apprenticeship programs to minorities. Home owners worry even more about profits, sales, commissions, and capital gains, and even less about school budgets. The respectable become particularly susceptible to drives against welfare "cheaters" and conjectural hordes of able-bodied loafers on the public dole. As they did in the 1950s, economists discover all over again that lots of people are simply unemployable, so that 5 to 6 percent unemployment is not something to be alarmed about. The unemployed are dumb, illiterate, immoral, lazy, or some unattractive combination of these qualities. From time to time Administration economists suggest that to be young or female is an additional justification for unemployment. CEA chairman Herbert Stein has confided to readers that the misery component of unemployment among youths and women is less than a similar incidence of joblessness among male heads of families.

Recession, especially during a conservative Administration, stimulates the tendency, seldom long dormant, to blame the victim.* If the unemployment and deprivation of recession are too expensive to alleviate—well then, why not revise the targets of employment policy? As the 1973 *Economic Report of the President* amiably phrased this position:

When the condition that persons who want work can find it through serious search is met, the rate of unemployment as we

---

*The phrase is William Ryan's. See his *Blaming the Victim* (New York: Pantheon, 1971).

measure it will not be zero. What it would be we do not know. Undoubtedly the number would change from time to time. But it is the condition which is important, not the statistic.

After all, who knows how many people are lazy?

3.

As true believers in Chicago and its ideological outposts in Virginia and California still hold, economists in general used to argue that the single source of inflation was excessive demand—usually, though not invariably, generated by the fiscal imprudence of spendthrift politicians. In the free markets of the economists' fancies, inflation led to recession, and recession speedily corrected the excesses and distortions of inflation.

In the ordered universe of the economic texts, wages and prices were flexible—downward as well as upward. When the customers stayed out of the stores and inventories began to pile up, prudent merchants ran genuine bargain sales. They also shrank their orders of new merchandise. Their suppliers, accordingly, made price concessions to the retailers. At each post on the economic battlefront, businessmen paid extra heed to the shifting pattern of consumer preference and responded with extra speed and precision to signals from the buyers. Their general reluctance to purchase translated throughout the price system as the occasion for general slashes in prices. The mechanism was not necessarily gentle. The less alert and less efficient were cast into the commercial darkness of bankruptcy. Their fate, however, taught a hard lesson. Where competition is king, the strong and efficient eliminate the weak and inefficient— to the benefit of the larger community.

It was essential to the expeditious completion of these

market adjustments that wages be as responsive to altered circumstances as prices. The argument was symmetrical. An hour or week of a man's labor has a price, just like a bank loan or a color television set. Rational independent employees and rational union leaders will recognize that when employers want fewer employees (because the customers want less, at existing prices, of what the employees turn out), then the sensible response is to offer one's services at reduced rates of compensation.

For the sellers of merchandise, the promised reward was renewed customer interest and larger sales. For the sellers of labor services, the reward was more jobs. The compelling principle at work was competition. Merchants had to match their rivals' prices on pain of losing their customers and in short order their properties. Present and potential employees are engaged in similar rivalries. Seeking to enlist new hands, employers prefer to hire, other things being equal, at lower rather than higher wage rates. Hesitating in slack times about layoffs, employers will refrain if workers accept wage cuts. As lower prices revive sales, lower wages revive employment. Recovery is the reward of virtue. In short order, the economy climbs out of its slough of despond and rises to the promised land of boom.

In this fable, the role of government is for the most part exemplary and heuristic. Preferring private to public activity, a sensible President and an intelligent Congress will work in harness to enlarge private competitive activity and shrink the size of the public sector. Internationally they would float the dollar in currency markets and move toward completely free trade. One can't have too much competition. Their budgetary policy should emphasize the desirability of annual balance between income and outlay. Balanced budgets encourage efficient use of tax money and check the extravagance of the bureaucrats. They also serve the cause of price stability. Ideally, monetary policy should also be neutral. A good rule is year-to-year expansion of money and credit at the same rate as the real growth of Gross National Product.

During times of recession, governments which adhere to the free-market principle will keep their cool and wait for competitive adjustments to work themselves out and recovery naturally to ensue. The adjustments will be made and the recovery will follow on schedule if the politicians keep their mouths shut and their clumsy hands off delicate economic mechanisms.

For better or worse, the real world is different. In it, the Penn Central goes broke but no one contemplates shutting it down. How else will wheat for Russian bread get loaded onto cargo vessels? How else can the Midwest ship Detroit autos, Grand Rapids furniture, and Wisconsin breakfast cereal to Eastern markets? In 1971 when Lockheed teetered on bankruptcy's brink, Congress voted it a special loan. As Secretary of the Treasury, John Connally defended the loan as a life preserver for jobs and incomes.

Whatever became of the proclaimed efficiencies secured by the reallocation of resources from less to more efficient entrepreneurs?

The real world is so full of anticompetitive elements that it is difficult to choose one's illustrations. During 1969 and 1970, building-trade wages shot sharply upward, but unemployment in these same crafts ran steadily higher than unemployment in general. In New York City, firemen, policemen, teachers, and sanitation employees extracted lavish settlements from local politicians who preferred peace to municipal solvency. These settlements were consummated during a spell of recession, teacher surplus, and severe restraint upon tax revenues.

Behavior on the price side is equally perverse. Between July 1952 and July 1957, finished steel prices rose 45 percent. During this half decade, the anti-inflationary Eisenhower policies limited wholesale prices in general to a mere 6 percent jump. Moreover, American steel plants were operating at low percentage of capacity, Japanese and German competitors and domestic steel substitutes like plastics and reinforced concrete were reducing the market opportunities likely to be available, and the American steel industry was rapidly losing its market advantages. Nevertheless, the leaders of the major steel firms stubbornly chose higher prices and lower sales in preference to lower prices, higher sales, and larger market shares.

Government seldom accommodates itself to the counsel of free-market theorists even when they officially advise conservative Presidents. The current energy crisis derives partly from the capacity of the Middle Eastern cartel of oil producers to limit pumping from its rich reserves and raise its prices to Japan, Western Europe, and the United States, at the time much less expensive than it later became. But government policy has contributed its bit. Thus, early in the first Nixon Administration, a Cabinet committee chaired by George Shultz recommended that oil quotas be eliminated. These quotas protected Texas oil magnates against competition from cheaper foreign oil. Natural-gas producers have deliberately restricted exploration for new sources as a pressure tactic calculated to lift federal price controls. A resolute free-market Administration would in short order have initiated antitrust action. Belatedly, in April 1973, the President came around to accepting the 1969 Shultz committee recommendation against quotas.

By the Administration's own estimates (which are unlikely to be reckless on such a point), oil and gas quotas have been costing Americans something like $5 billion annually, rather more than the President proposed to spend on the welfare reforms included in the now abandoned Family Assistance Plan. Washington's generosity is not limited to mineral extraction. The cost of living soared in 1973 as a result of President Nixon's romance with the farm vote in his first term. Until the autumn of 1972, the Department of Agriculture administered severe acreage restrictions on planting and provided generous subsidies to farmers, particularly needy large operators like Senator James Eastland of Mississippi.

Wherever government intervenes, its actions are far more likely to restrict than enlarge competition and to raise instead of lowering prices. In the regulated industries—transportation, telephones, gas, and electricity—federal agencies and their much feebler state colleagues have in the past acted as indulgent friends of the industries they ostensibly regulate. No more in the present than in the past do the regulators vigorously defend consumer interests. In the last six years, hospital costs (strongly influenced by Medicare and Medicaid subsidies) have doubled. Late in 1972 they averaged a startling $105.30 daily for a semiprivate room. In New York City, the Citizens Union Research Foundation estimated that policemen and firemen with thirty years of service and currently earning $16,000 as final-year pay will receive pension benefits amounting to $9,900 annually for twenty-four years at a total cost to less fortunate New Yorkers of $237,600 per pensioner. Although there are dangers to their jobs, a man of average intelligence and physique, equipped with a high school diploma, can easily qualify for membership in the uniformed services —and the benefits thereof.

What public agencies fail to do is frequently as significant as their sins of commission. Refusal to promote oil and gas exploration on public lands props up domestic fuel prices. Cozy consent-decree arrangements between the Department of Justice and large corporations inhibits the development of new antitrust laws. Rigid civil service rules limit job competition by the inadequately credentialed.

Universities and professional societies should protect the public against charlatans. Often they operate less in the public than in the private interest and according to the model of the more exclusive construction crafts. Doctors and university professors raise ever higher credentials barriers to protect their own income. No-fault liability has been delayed for years by trial lawyers who have profited from the prosecution of negligence suits. Nursing associations insist upon four years of college, although no one has demonstrated that the professional skills and emotional empathy required of the good nurse are closely related to a college degree. Dental hygienists must meet training requirements rather than performance standards. Skilled medical specialists perform routine tasks at splendid fees which otherwise might as efficiently be completed by semiskilled technicians more humbly compensated.

These are a very few examples of an army of restrictions upon entry into unions and professions, special benefits to well-organized interests, tariffs and quotas, subsidies to defense contractors, indulgent regulation of public utilities, raids by municipal unions on city treasuries, monopoly positions in industry, insurance, and finance, and miscellaneous extortions from the unprotected portions of the community. It is not an exaggeration to assert that wherever an observer's eye falls, it registers a situation of market control or actual dominance by a small number of individuals, corporations, health insurers, trade unions, business associations, or professional societies. In manufacturing, since 1966 the largest 200 corporations have raised their share of the sector's total assets from 57 to 66 percent. These mighty 200 are one tenth of one percent of the 200,000 corporations in business.*

In other respects, life for monopolists has in recent years become happier and happier. The oil producers of the Middle East, otherwise united only in their hatred of Israel, have learned the delights of cooperation. The oil producers' cartel has already extracted higher royalties from the American and European oil companies. American mismanagement of our own fuel resources will no doubt very soon vastly enlarge the cartel's collection of tribute and, inevitably, serve as sufficient reason to raise gasoline and heating-oil prices still further.

The generally backward rulers of the Persian Gulf have been presented with enormous sums of money, which they are disinclined to apply to the modernization of their own fiefs. Instead they have discovered that the thrills of international currency speculation are even more fun than the gambling casinos of Monte Carlo. The second recent devaluation of the dollar appears to have been accelerated and conceivably even caused by use of oil royalties to buy German marks and sell United States dollars. The sheiks' decision, utterly beyond the control of the Federal Reserve or any other American authority, rearranged the relationship of dollars to marks and yen, and operated as an additional source of inflationary pressure. For devaluation raised the prices in the United States of imported fuel, raw materials, and consumer goods, drove the consumer price index still higher, automatically increased wages tied by union contracts to movements in that index, and stimulated foreign demand for American raw materials and finished goods. As a result, domestic supplies shrank, their prices rose, and poorer Americans

---

*The estimates are those of Dr. Willard Mueller, former chief economist of the Federal Trade Commission.

were compelled to buy less and shift to inferior substitutes.

As raw materials become increasingly scarce and American resources are consumed,* the temptations of monopoly are bound to spread from oil producers to miners of chrome, copper, tin, nickel, uranium, and other useful metals. Almost regardless of the wisdom or folly of American leaders, inflationary pressure from this source will mount. Checking it may require either a major recession or a vast reordering of the manner in which Americans organize their lives.

In the meantime we should take what comfort we can from the words of Saudi Arabia's minister of petroleum, Sheik Ahmed Zaki Yamani: "Saudi Arabia will be a paradise in ten or twenty years." Why not? His country is inhabited by a sparse 8.2 million persons and endowed by Allah with 145 billion barrels of oil reserves. From its wells, Saudi Arabia pumps a mere 6 million barrels daily and enjoys annual oil revenues of $2.3 billion. Matters are even better arranged in Libya, a desert occupied by about 2 million men and women. Its income from oil is $1.6 billion, a much pleasanter per capita sum. Kuwait, population 800,000, is paid $1.1 billion for its oil.

The total population of the seven large Arab oil producers is under 52 million and their total oil receipts in 1972 touched the $10 billion mark. Prophecy is general that within a few years, they will double or triple this sum. How the wicked do flourish if they live on oil-soaked sand!

The Arab countries are independent sovereignties into whose decisions it is geographically inconven-

*Each year Americans use up *40 percent* of the world's output of raw materials, an appalling testimonial to the cult of the car and the national appetite for packaged merchandise.

ient* for American military power to intervene, especially because Soviet-American détente could scarcely bear the strain. The Russians too have Middle Eastern interests and clients.

There are other powers and principalities which, although legally less independent, appear in operation nearly as much beyond the control of elected officials as Sheik Yamani and his associates. These of course are the multinational corporations whose operations in many countries take place outside the commercial law of any one or several of their hosts. Events in Chile, San Diego, Washington, D.C. and elsewhere have made Harold Geneen's gigantic corporate child, International Telephone & Telegraph, the most famous of all these goliaths. In 1970 ITT did business in seventy countries, sold $2.7 billion outside of the United States, and collected $123.6 million in foreign earnings, over a third of total profit from all its operations.

ITT has company. In the course of activities spread over the globe, Standard Oil (N.J.) did $8.3 billion in foreign business and earned profits of $681.2 million from these sales—more than half of its total earnings. The multinationals include other major oil companies: Dow Chemical; Honeywell, IBM, and Xerox among the office-machine and computer magnates; Ford and General Motors; jacks-of-all-trade like Litton Industries and Grace; and food producers on the order of Coca-Cola, General Foods, and Swift.†

The companies range from discreet to flamboyant in styles of maneuver. ITT is everybody's favorite illustration of the latter. At home ITT combined generous campaign contributions with high-level political lobbying in

---

*But by no means impossible, as the Marine landing on the beaches of Lebanon during the 1950s attests.
†See *Dun's* (April 1973), p. 43.

order to preserve its vital acquisition of the Hartford Fire
Insurance Company. As former Attorney General John
Mitchell is supposed comfortingly to have assured Mr.
Geneen at a tense negotiating moment, "We don't think
bigness is bad." For ITT the story had a happy ending.
The case was settled out of court. ITT kept its insurance
company. The militant attorney who had taken the antitrust laws a trifle too seriously was quickly promoted to
the federal bench.

Abroad ITT conducted its own foreign policy. In 1970
its lobbyists were furiously engaged in trying to stop
Salvador Allende from becoming Chile's first Marxist
President. William Merriam, at the time head of ITT's
Washington office, described some of his activities in an
internal memo:

Today I had lunch with our contact at the McLean agency
[CIA] . . . Approaches continue to be made to select members
of the Armed Forces in an attempt to have them lead some sort
of uprising—no success to date. In the meantime Allende continues to hold meetings with small groups of army, navy, and
air force people promising them, personally that he will see to
it that they will be promoted; that their pay will be increased,
etc. Thus it is easy to see where there is a problem in getting
the military to take action.

In desperation ITT sent John McCone, one of its di-
rectors and a former head of the CIA, to Richard Helms,
his successor, with an offer of up to $1 million to finance
any dirty trick which would depose Allende. Although
the CIA appears to have rejected this gesture of altruism,
Helms did instruct a subordinate, William Broe, to con-
fer with Geneen. At this meeting, several months before
the Chilean election, Broe was presented with a proposition to channel "a substantial sum" to Allende's conservative opponent, Jorge Alessandri Rodriguez.

With no special reaction of outrage, Broe replied,

"Well, I told him we could not absorb the funds and serve as a funding channel. I also told him that the United States government was not supporting any candidate in the Chilean election." A man of affairs, Broe was handicapped by no prim reluctance to intervene in the affairs of an independent nation. He helpfully supplied as a substitute for ITT's plan a list of five ways in which ITT and other American corporations of equally good will could concert their operations so as to create economic chaos and presumably damage Allende's prospects.

One need scarcely add that all these discussions among equals took place in an atmosphere of warm cordiality. In one ITT letter Vice-President Spiro Agnew is addressed as "Dear Ted" and thanked for his help in settling the firm's antitrust difficulties. The missive, which concludes with "I would appreciate your reaction on how we should proceed," is signed "Ned" by Edward Gerrit, an ITT vice-president. Similar communications feature "Dear Chuck" (Charles Colson), "Dear Pete" (Peter Peterson), and other Administration figures. Other memos feature "John" and "Hal"—Mitchell and Geneen. Under the circumstances, perhaps ITT might be forgiven for acting as an independent power to which it granted the Nixon Administration a status of equality.*

Only as ensuing scandals unfold will average plebeians be privileged to guess how typical these events are of the life and high old times of the multinationals. The picaresque story of Dita Beard, John Mitchell, Charles Colson, and their friends in Chilean and American politics is a good dirty story, a source of innocent merriment in a glum time.

Far more important than the dirty tricks is the sheer

*I have drawn upon a useful *New Republic* account in the periodical's issue of April 14, 1973, p. 5 and following.

economic weight and legal freedom which the multinationals now enjoy. It is possible though difficult to punish businessmen and officials whose conduct too outrageously offends law or public morals. The harder problems are structural.

As matters now stand, the multinationals are free to shift at will or whim manufacturing facilities, financial resources, and sales efforts from political jurisdiction to political jurisdiction. When Henry Ford II grows angry (with some reason) at the state of labor relations in Ford's Dagenham plant near London, he can plausibly threaten to relocate planned new English facilities to Belgium or Holland. Ford, General Motors, and Chrysler fabricate auto parts where labor is cheap, import them for use on assembly lines within the United States, and curtail purchases of American components. Or, the companies can readily increase imports of cars they assemble abroad and sell them in competition with United States–made models.

Strong unions, minimum-wage standards, occupational safety requirements, and social security protections increase the expense of hiring American workers. None or few of these meddlesome restrictions of managerial prerogative distress managers in Taiwan, South Korea, Hong Kong, and other low-wage Free World bastions. The capacity of the multinationals to play one country off against another, analogous to games mobile corporations play within the United States with industry-hungry states, threatens to damage the structure of worker protections laboriously erected within advanced Western societies in the two centuries since the English industrial revolution.

Much as they shuffle plants and facilities, multinationals transfer vast sums of money from one currency to another. The experts divide the blame (or credit) for 1973's dollar devaluation between the Arab oil producers and the American multinationals. Against these potentates, foreign and formally domestic, American monetary policy is virtually powerless. Operating solely upon domestic financial institutions, the Federal Reserve cannot prevent multinational firms from borrowing in Europe or Japan on occasions when the American central bankers discourage the same activity at home. It follows that the more successfully multinationals evade American credit controls, the more heavily will these controls be applied to targets who cannot escape—the traditional list of local governments, home buyers, installment-loan borrowers, and corporations domiciled entirely within the United States.

As the officials of the multinationals frequently point out, their earnings ultimately flow back as profits and dividends to the United States. It is equally certain that the capacity of these organizations to export jobs and facilities threatens domestic employment and existing protections of domestic working conditions. Their ability to export capital potentially enlarges short-run American international balance-of-payments deficits. Their access to foreign sources of capital shields them from the impact of monetary stringency in the United States. And their bewildering complexity of organization and operation in many jurisdictions protects them from effective regulation in any jurisdiction.

One should avoid exaggerating the combined results of these varied limitations of competition, for even among the concentrated industries there are traces of rivalry. The general hunt for consumer dollars by the purveyors of boats, cars, appliances, vacations in the sun, leisure clothing, fine wines, and restaurant meals serves as a mild check on the capacity of the most potent oligopolist to operate without regard for his immediate rivals and the possibility that the customers will turn fickle and shift their attention to entirely different products or services. Moreover, a sufficiently deep recession in time compels the least repentant corporate giant to reduce prices as a prop to faltering sales. Finally, in retailing and in a few areas of manufacturing something like old-fashioned price competition continues to reign.

This said, it is still the dominant fact of our economic organization that monetary and fiscal policies work only very slowly in the presence of concentrated market power in major industries, indulgent regulation of public utilities, and capital barriers to the entry of new firms, and union, professional society, and university barriers to job qualification. Federal, state, and local agencies abet private practice with tariffs, quotas, acreage restrictions, occupational licensing, and preferential treatment of the larger defense contractors.

Cost-push inflation is a shorthand summary of a condition in which a great many of the more important actors on the economic stage have learned how to prosper without competing. In the distance they hear the alarum bells rung by the Federal Reserve, but only slowly do they arrive at the conclusion that the bells ring for them. Far too long for the comfort of politicians and their constituents, the wielders of market power maintain or even increase their prices after the fashion of the steel industry during the crises, even in the face of declining sales. Construction unions ultimately accept the wage implications of recession in building. "Ultimately" may mean several years during which their leaders continue to push wage rates still higher.

When cost-push inflation occurs, wages and prices become flexible only in an upward direction. Cost-push imparts a permanent inflationary bias to the economy and it imposes severe limitations on the efficacy of conventional tools of budgetary and monetary policy.

III.
What Can
Be Done?

For Presidents and their agents, the easiest economic response to inflation is represented by the wisdom of Dickens' Micawber—do nothing and wait for something to turn up. The lure of inactivity is the more attractive because, as what follows will explain, there are *no* easy reconciliations of high employment and low prices in semicompetitive, quasi-monopolistic, "free" market economies. All policies impose costs and contain benefits. Political risk is implicit in any approach to the dilemmas of intervention.

In his first two years President Nixon seemed to pursue a Micawberite policy, until the political time clock began to run down. In 1973 the Chief Executive appeared to be repeating this initial strategy. As CEA chairman Herbert Stein phrased the eternal philosophy: ". . . I think it [Phase III] will be a success. But, I believe that a judgment at this time is premature. . . . we will not be able to evaluate Phase 3 until many years after it is dead, and we can see what its legacy has been."*

*From a speech delivered to the American Statistical Association, April 20, 1973, at the New York Hilton, p. 1 (mimeographed).

To hope that something will turn up is to expect that present policy will end in success. It is always possible to assert that loose controls are adequate if unions are patient, businessmen do not get carried away by record-breaking sales and profits,* customers refrain from buying absolutely everything in sight on easy installments,† Congress patriotically enacts the President's budget, and above all, the great public believes what Mr. Nixon and his economic advisers tell them about the wisdom of present monetary, fiscal, and control policies. In the Age of Watergate, the last condition may be the most difficult of all to fulfill.

Watergate aside, Americans are impatient folk who on the historical record will take the long view of their economic troubles only when the President happens to be a well-loved national hero like Dwight Eisenhower or a young prince like John F. Kennedy. Seedier performers, like Lyndon Johnson and Richard Nixon, are required to produce speedier results. Lovable they never were. Efficient they must be perceived to be, on pain of desertion by their calculating supporters. Average Presidents become, even if they begin otherwise, economic activists.

A President can be active in one or more of four ways. A Chief Executive who believes in free markets both for their own beauties and for their relation to price stability will pursue the implications of his faith. Genuine old-fashioned price competition is incompatible with giant corporations and national trade unions. In the American economy as we know it, large corporations are private

---

*Profits in the first three months of 1973 were 23 percent higher than in the corresponding period of the preceding year, and 6.6 percent greater than the record $57.2 billion rate recorded in the final three months of 1972. See *Business Week* (May 12, 1973), p. 91.

†By April 1973 Americans were borrowing at an annual rate of $24 billion, up from $13 billion at the start of 1972. The ratio of debt to disposable income was 2.8 percent—an all-time high. *Ibid.*, p. 38.

price controllers who also share control over wage rates with the major unions. So long as these corporations and unions dominate their markets, prices and wages are certain to move only upward. It follows that a true-blue free market ideologue cannot logically stop short of breaking up General Motors and the lesser goliaths celebrated each June by *Fortune* magazine's list of 500 major industrial corporations. Imagine an economy in which each GM, Ford, and Chrysler assembly plant operated as an independent entity. When business was slow and the customers stayed away from the auto showrooms, a hundred or more auto companies would surely compete among themselves by cutting their prices, as four companies currently do not. Prices which, in economic parlance, are now flexible only upward, would become flexible downward as well. A similar prescription applies to national unions. Local unions, whose memberships were limited to the employees of single plants, would bargain with equally weak employers. Wages would also become flexible downward. In such a universe, tax spending and banking interventions by Washington become less necessary because sellers raise their prices only when business is good, and rapidly expand output as a limitation upon further price increases. In slack times, price and wage cuts swiftly restore markets for goods and labor services. On the occasions when monetary and fiscal interventions are undertaken by the Federal Reserve and the Treasury, corporations and unions respond alertly to the Washington signals.

Despite the political pitfalls, already identified, of combining inflation and unemployment, a President may prefer to endure protracted recession as the only sure means of wringing inflationary expectations out of large corporations, unions, and ordinary consumers. If pursued with sufficient resolution for a sufficient period of time, monetary restraint is a policy which, at the cost of much lost output and new unemployment, does slow wage and price acceleration.

Unwilling or politically unable to accept or persevere in either of these strategies, a Chief Executive can accept inflation as a fact of life and adapt the economy to a situation of permanent inflation.

There is a final course of action. A national administration might respond to the concentration of economic power not by busting trusts and unions but by accepting the necessity of permanent controls by government over the private exercise of concentrated economic power.

2.

As the most venerable of interventionist policies, anti-trust deserves pride of place. Made into law in 1890, the Sherman Act preaches two articles of market theology:

Section 1.   Every contract, combination in the form of trust or otherwise, or conspiracy in restraint of trade or commerce among the several States or with foreign nations, is hereby declared to be illegal. . . .

Section 2.   Every person who shall monopolize, or attempt to monopolize, or combine or conspire with any other person or persons, to monopolize any part of the trade or commerce among the several States, or with foreign nations, shall be deemed guilty of a misdemeanor.

Congress underlined its detestation of monopolies and restraints of trade during Woodrow Wilson's New Freedom. In 1914 it passed two landmark statutes. The Clayton Act declared the illegality of four popular restrictive practices—price discrimination, exclusive dealing and tying contracts, acquisition of competitors, and interlocking directorates. Congress also established the Federal Trade Commission to extirpate "Unfair methods of competition in commerce and unfair or deceptive acts or practices in commerce."

This country is the proprietor of the most powerful arsenal of legal tools against monopoly and assorted anticompetitive practices in the civilized world. It is the law of the land that corporate executives who flagrantly breach the antitrust laws risk jail sentences. Their corporations are subject to large fines and instructions in future to behave themselves better. Courts on occasion command companies to divest themselves of subsidiaries when present ownership menaces competition.

It would be cynical to argue that the penalties have the same effect on conduct as the New Testament has on Republican politics. Once in a while a courageous judge takes the antitrust laws seriously. Thus, in 1962 a Philadelphia federal judge actually sentenced a group of General Electric and Westinghouse officials to short jail terms for their role in an extensive price-fixing conspiracy. These pillars of the community actually served twenty-one days.* In the 1970s, newspaper reporters linger considerably longer when they refuse to reveal the sources of their information. And although the electrical-equipment overcharges ran into the tens of millions of dollars and stimulated a rash of private litigation against General Electric and the other offenders, run-of-the-mill embezzlers are far more severely treated.

In business circles the felonious executives were viewed as martyrs rather than criminals. At worst their offense was poor business judgment, at least in the eyes of their peers. Over the years the Department of Justice has rarely brought criminal charges against respectable businessmen. It has preferred amicable negotiation with

---

*The terms were set at thirty days. Nine days were remitted for good behavior.

antitrust offenders, or consent decrees which protect corporations from damage suits and spare them the embarrassments of revelation in open court. Once in a while corporations are required to spin off one of their divisions. Rather more frequently they are urged to stop doing something which is too outrageously anticompetitive. As always, antitrust offers lucrative employment to lawyers on all sides of the issues.

A generation ago Thurman Arnold sharply judged that "The actual result of the antitrust laws was to promote the growth of great industrial organizations by deflecting the attack on them into purely moral and ceremonial channels." The late Richard Hofstadter, a historian of the Progressive era, described antitrust as a "faded passion of American reform." Both of these astute observers were recording a fact of American life: a good blast against monopoly entertains the populace and does no harm to the monopolists. A genuine attempt to break up major unions and giant corporations is, one guesses, approximately as popular as school busing in Detroit and scatter-site housing in Queens. On the record, Americans are simply too fond of big business and too used to the AFL-CIO to seriously envisage the disruptions attendant upon real application of the antitrust statutes. This is of course good news for both major parties, whose political campaigns are financed mostly from corporation and union treasuries.

There is little question that antitrust is better economics than it is politics. Monopoly and oligopoly* really do raise prices, reduce output and employment, and complicate monetary and fiscal policy. Economists are boring and repetitive but probably correct in teaching their stu-

---

*Oligopoly is the shared control of a major industry, exemplified in automobiles by General Motors, Ford, and Chrysler. It is the dominant pattern of manufacturing organization.

dents that markets operate with maximum efficiency only in the presence of genuine price rivalry. This rivalry maximizes pressure upon costs, encourages innovation, and compels sellers and producers to respond quickly and accurately to the registered preferences of their customers.

Monopoly is as economically undesirable as it is legally reprehensible. As an intellectual exercise, it is worth exploring the features of an intelligent antitrust program. Its starting point is recognition that bigness by itself, John Mitchell to the contrary notwithstanding, menaces competition, quite aside from the commission of specifically illegal acts by responsible corporate executives. However sincerely the leaders of General Motors believe in their own speeches on the virtues of competition, they cannot but know that an industry of three giants and American Motors sets prices of new models as deliberate policy. False modesty is unlikely to conceal from Richard Gerstenberg, GM's chairman, that it is his company which determines the prices that the smaller auto goliaths perforce accept.*

The existence of General Motors offends the notion of free competition. True believers consequently must favor fragmentation of GM into a hundred or more pieces that competition may once again flower. So also for Ford and Chrysler and the huge corporations which dominate steel, rubber, chemicals, aluminum, and other oligopo-

---

*In the first quarter of 1973, GM's net income was $816.5 million earned from sales of $9.57 *billion*. During this period GM sold 2,403,000 cars and trucks, assembling 1,822,000 in the United States and the remainder in Canada or overseas. As an economic entity GM is far larger than most of the members of the United Nations. Such a superpower perforce behaves politically as much as economically. It cannot neglect the impact of its decisions on a labor force approaching a million persons, the communities and countries where it locates its facilities, and the politicians who occupy influential positions. None of these matters concerns the small operators of classical theory, because each one is too weak to exercise general influence.

lized industries. As economists now and again observe, bigger does not necessarily mean more efficient. If it were really the case that GM grew to its present size because of the technical economies of scale, then it would assemble its cars and trucks in a single plant rather than in dozens of facilities scattered over the globe. Other economies of scale—financial, advertising, and marketing—are at least partly offset by the bureaucratic inefficiencies attendant upon large size. Few of the gains which remain are passed on to the customers in the shape of lower prices. The beneficiaries are the managers and stockholders. Thus, technically at least, nothing much would be lost by a declaration of organizational independence for each separate factory. *A fortiori* a similar judgment applies to GM's important nonautomotive operations.

Consistent dissolution of giant corporations on the basis of their size, not their conduct, would restructure industry and finance.* Among its incidental effects, it would throw television and marketing into turmoil. When *Fortune*'s 500 biggest industrials are dissolved, who will sponsor professional sports and Republican presidential candidates? Where will the graduates of Harvard Law School and the Harvard School of Business work when, like dinosaurs, the oligopolists move off the stage of evolution?

Such is the first portion of a free-market program. Next tariffs, quotas, and subsidies to shipbuilders, corporate farmers, oil operators, land developers, and defense contractors would be swept away. Their impact on competition is malign. The foreign products excluded by trade barriers are likely to be higher in quality or lower

---

*Utilities might be spared on the ground that their technology justifies natural monopoly. New Yorkers find Consolidated Edison hard to bear. They would suffer still more from a dozen Con Ed's each busily ripping up the streets.

in price than their less attractive American substitutes. American consumers, therefore, subsidize less efficient native producers. Because of marine subsidies, approximately five hundred merchant vessels sail under the American flag. In the absence of the subsidies, the most efficient one hundred might survive.

The laws which regulate union activity and professional licensing also urgently cry for dramatic revision. In 1973 American circumstances, powerful national unions amount to a natural and wholesome response to similar concentrations of employer power. But the demise of national corporations argues for the dissolution of national unions and substitution of local unions parallel in structure to the industries they bargain with. Otherwise unions would turn into powerful agents of inflation, able to win all their battles against much weaker employers.

Licensing is apparently a different matter. For obvious reasons, doctors and lawyers should, by community preference, be competent. Physical and fiscal life or death is the stuff of their daily labors. Patients like to think that their surgeons' steady fingers cut away minimum quantities of healthy tissue and remove malignancies entire. On the whole, they prefer that the medical profession exclude drunks, drug addicts, victims of Parkinson's disease, and professionally backward types. At a minimum, lawyers ought to be acquainted with relevant law, handle their clients' money honestly, and file legal papers on time. Similar judgments apply to dentists, engineers, architects, nurses, and teachers.

Granted. Unfortunately, actual licensing is a once-for-all procedure which evaluates novices severely (or indulgently) only at the start of their professional careers. Short of extreme misconduct, outrageous incompetence, or outright criminality, lawyers are not disbarred, doctors struck from the medical register, or teachers barred from the classrooms where they bore their victims into intellectual apathy.

A few consistent free-market intellectuals, following the lead of Dr. Milton Friedman, have maintained that since licensing mainly serves to protect members of the licensed profession against unsanctioned competition, the sensible thing to do is abolish it completely. Let who wants to set himself up in legal, medical, or pedagogical practice. The free-enterprise position appears, at a minimum, to require licensing by authorities who represent customers as well as professional suppliers, and periodic review by such authorities of the professional competence of their charges.

Freer entry into professions and crafts is not the end of the structural changes needed to restore (or create) a free-market economy. A number of traditional government functions require reconsideration. The financial cards are now, for example, stacked in favor of public schools. Although parents are free to send their progeny to independent or religious schools, they must as taxpayers also support public schools for the benefit of families which prefer them or can afford no alternative. An approximation of a free educational market would be created by distribution to parents of vouchers whose cash value was the locality's average per-child public-school outlays. The vouchers could then be used to enroll a youngster in any accredited school—private, religious, or public. Schools perforce would compete for patronage, and shrink or expand according to the taste of their patrons.

In principle, medical and housing vouchers might supplement the more familiar educational version. Under present arrangements, low-income families are forced to enjoy public subsidy in the shape of public housing, when it is available at all. Why not broaden their choice with housing vouchers usable in private as well as public housing? Medical vouchers would similarly enlarge patients' opportunities to select voluntary instead of public hospitalization.

The reordered economy here sketched would be much less subject to inflationary pressure than the economy with which Americans are familiar. Prices, wages, fees, and medical charges would be far more responsive than they are now to the influence of shifting tastes or vigorous new competitors. Free trade across national borders further enlarges this flexibility. Guaranteed open access to American markets, foreigners would surely cultivate American tastes even more forcefully than is their present habit. Although neither recession nor inflation would be scourged from the land, both would be briefer and less severe.

I have lingered so long on this design less because of its realistic prospects than because of the intellectual strength of the free-market case. Americans will be ready for free markets on the day when the National Association of Manufacturers concedes that bigness is bad, farmers conclude that price supports are enemies of freedom, the American Medical Association insists that doctors be periodically examined for reaccreditation by boards that include public members, the American Bar Association argues for regular purges of its incompetent, undependable, or senile members, the American Association of University Professors discovers that tenure damages efficient teaching, George Meany sets a ceiling on the size of each union, politicians decide to finance their campaigns out of the small, voluntary contributions of average constituents, defense contractors proudly assert that bankruptcy in the cause of freedom is no shame, and the American public, no fools, concludes that there is a genuine chance to make headway against the formidable coalition of the entrenched that these interests comprise.

In the light of the dim prospect that these events will come to pass, it is perhaps reassuring to record that not all economists would, if they could, fragment large corporations and restore free markets. The late Adolf Berle and his follower (on this topic) J. K. Galbraith have identified the large corporation as the dominant economic institution of the century. According to Galbraith, technological progress has been most pronounced in oligopolistic industries and least noticeable where competition is keenest. From this proposition, Berle and Galbraith inferred another: corporations should be accepted but civilized. Probably a majority of economists are convinced neither by the Galbraithians nor the free-marketeers. They simply, as practical souls, tremble at the dislocations which radical antitrust implies. Since the political outlook is dim, economists prefer to spend their time on other matters.

As usual, the realists have the best of the immediate argument. It is, all the same, hard not to shed a tear for free markets. Anyone worried about concentrated power and distressed by the suitcases of cash which traveled from multinational conglomerates and domestic oligopolists to the Committee for the Re-election of the President might well wonder whether the society wouldn't be healthier and its politicians honester if money and power were less concentrated.

3.

For now familiar reasons, recession is politically more painful than it was in the nineteenth century, when it could be blamed on God or the moral failures of laborers and businessmen. Recession may nevertheless be economically unavoidable for political communities which are unwilling to embrace substantial structural change. Can recession be made tolerable?

Joined to the permanent inflationary biases in our economy is considerable variability in the spending behavior of consumers and investors. The 1973 *Economic Report of the President* predicted in that year a real growth of GNP (after eliminating the effect of inflation) of 6.75 percent. On the average, prices were supposed to rise 3 percent and drop by year's end to 2.5 percent. Yet by April 1973, three months after the *Economic Report* surfaced, real GNP was rising at 8 percent and prices were climbing at a perilous 6 percent clip. Why were the consumers spending more than the experts predicted? Were they anticipating still more inflation and spending their money before it lost more of its value?

The behavior of investors is even more volatile. As Keynes memorably noted in the 1930s, businessmen decide to buy new equipment and construct new factories not because they can predict the future, but because they feel cheerful about it. Investment was a product of the "animal spirits" of the business community, their euphoric picture of the unknowable years ahead. In 1973 the animal spirits of American businessmen were demonstrably bounding. A huge investment boom complemented a wild consumer outburst and generated a pattern of growth which could not for very long be sustained, simply because shortages of raw materials, plant facilities, and ultimately human labor were bound to bring it to a stop.

Save for its scale, 1973's boom was far from unprecedented. Investment has long been cyclical. Changes in its level have always generated magnified effects on income and spending. When consumers simultaneously reduce saving and enlarge buying, demand-pull inflation reappears. If untreated and unchecked, its consequences soon include supply bottlenecks, spreading inefficiencies of production and distribution, and mounting customer resistance to sour combinations of poor service, declining quality, and escalating prices. In short order, sobering reality dashes unrealistic profit predictions, inflated anticipations of capital gains from real property and stock equities, and utopian wage gains. Though recession is frequently an act of central-banking policy, it is also an affliction of disappointed hope and dashed greed. The most imprudent or the most unlucky go broke. Chastened survivors shave investment plans. Consumers, after the ball is over, return from the showrooms and department stores to savings banks and experiments with private canning and sewing.

Politicians who allow inflation to get well started are shortly confronted with unpleasant choices. If they clamp on the monetary brakes and raise taxes, they will stop economic expansion in its tracks and cool inflation at the price of deliberate recession. Early action of this kind at best offers the chance of a relatively mild and brief recession, followed by new expansion on a less feverish basis. It is easier for Presidents and members of Congress to delay higher taxes and interest rates, which are never popular with their constituents. But the longer inflation and economic expansion continue, the harder it is to check its course and the more likely it must be that once the monetary and fiscal authorities do act, the resulting recession will be severe. Recession now? Recession later? These are the gloomy alternatives. Tight money can dash a great many hopes in relatively short order. Recession, we have complained, is a phenomenon endured by the poor for the benefit of the prosperous, or at least the cannier among them. Why should blacks and women, low on seniority ladders and innocent of responsibility for inflation, be forced to pay in unemployment the costs of cooling the boom? Why should welfare mothers be told to find work at precisely the time when jobs are scarcest?

It should be possible to protect vulnerable individuals with no greater difficulty than Lockheed and Litton are now spared the consequences of managerial inefficiency and financial folly. Why not, as Galbraith long ago proposed,* tie unemployment compensation to the rate of unemployment and the stage of the business cycle. The more depressed the economy, the higher the unemployment rate, and the more generous the scale of payment to the jobless. No danger here to the work ethic, since general economic adversity, not individual moral failure, was manifestly at work.

Of course it would be still more enlightened to provide useful work for the victims of recession. A generously conceived and funded program of public-service employment has the merit at once of preserving the skills and dignity of those who get the jobs and of creating for public enjoyment and utility a variety of educational, health, sanitary, and recreational opportunities. In the 1970s as in the 1950s, the United States is a land of private affluence set in public squalor. Galbraith's ode continues to be pertinent:

The family which takes its mauve and cerise, air-conditioned, power-steered, and power-braked automobile out for a tour passes through cities that are badly paved, made hideous by litter, blighted buildings, billboards, and posts for wires that should long since have been put underground. They pass on into a countryside that has been rendered largely invisible by commercial art. (The goods which the latter advertise have an absolute priority in our value system. Such aesthetic considerations as a view of countryside accordingly come second. On such matters we are consistent.) They picnic on exquisitely packaged food from a portable icebox by a polluted stream and go on to spend the night at a park which is a menace to public health and morals. Just before dozing off on an air mattress, beneath a nylon tent, amid the stench of decaying refuse, they may reflect vaguely on the curious unevenness of their blessings. Is this, indeed, the American genius?†

*See his *American Capitalism* (Boston: Houghton Mifflin, 1952).
†See *The Affluent Society* (Boston: Houghton Mifflin, 1958), p. 253.

In the 1970s, as in the past, cities are underpoliced, patients in public hospitals get sicker because there are too few nurses, doctors, and attendants, and class sizes edge upward in ghetto schools whose pupils desperately require personal attention. The failures are of social sympathy rather than of technique. One of the more cheerful but underfinanced experiments of the 1960s involved the employment of paraprofessional aides drawn from the communities in which they worked. In the schools these aides, usually female heads of families of sketchy formal education, have provided not only assistance to regular teachers but jobs and hope for the paraprofessionals, and warmth and affection for the children.

More money could sensibly be devoted in more places to the employment of school paraprofessionals. Moreover, the model is transferable to other human services. Where it has been tried, results have been promising for the paraprofessionals, their clients, and the institutions themselves in a variety of activities. Legal paraprofessionals operating out of legal-services offices have grappled sensitively with the concerns of their neighbors. Opportunities for medical auxiliaries in hospitals, clinics, and public-health services are exceedingly numerous.

In its human aspects, the service society* is meagerly supported. As a matter of course, more resources ought to be devoted to the healing and helping activities which the private sector fails to distribute to less affluent citizens. A recession is a particularly opportune moment to fill social need and pursue correct economic policy simultaneously.

The political omens have not recently been propitious.

---

*The United States is the first society in the world to employ more members of its labor force producing services rather than goods.

In 1971, over President Nixon's opposition, Congress enacted the Emergency Employment Act, which for the entire country appropriated enough money to hire 150,000 persons in state and local agencies. As Washington counts the unemployed, some five million people were at the time looking for jobs. If account were taken of disheartened men and women who had stopped searching for unavailable employment,* underemployed persons, and individuals compelled to operate beneath their skill level, the five-million figure would, conservatively speaking, double. A strange communal blindness is at work when a society refuses to relate unfilled public needs to the unemployed men and women who are eager to meet them.

What could the President and Congress have done in the 1969–1970 recession to combine the control of inflation with fair treatment of the victims of their policy? Once it was obvious that unemployment was certain to rise, Congress and President should have joined in a program of public-job creation instead of waiting until recovery had begun to set in. The action itself should have been both more generous and less ambiguous in tone than the Emergency Employment Act. Not only was the number of jobs allowed by the act grossly inadequate to the size of the problem, but the statute misguidedly stressed recession as the only justification of new funding for local services. In the language of its preamble, the act aimed "To provide *during times of high unemployment* programs of public service employment for unemployed

---

*The Bureau of Labor Statistics excludes from the labor force, and hence does not count among the unemployed, anyone who in the preceding thirty days has not actively sought employment. No account is taken of the possibility (probability?) that a person who has looked unsuccessfully for a job during a six-, nine-, or twelve-month period is at some point facing reality when he looks no longer.

persons to assist States and local communities in providing needed public services [Emphasis added]." Recalling Calvin Coolidge's insight that when people are out of work, unemployment results, the drafters of the bill noted that "in times of high unemployment, many low-income persons are unable to secure or to retain employment." Throughout, possibly to avert presidential veto and probably to soothe congressional conservatives, stress was heavy upon the transitional character of the new jobs, the preferability of private-sector employment, and the temporary nature of the problem, and hence, the statute.

Congress thus evaded a major social point: the permanent need to enlarge the availability of the human services which are largely supported in the public sector. A recession, from this perspective, is an extra opportunity to rectify the Galbraithian imbalance between private plenty and public poverty. The moral is plain: it *is* possible to civilize recession and convert the need to cool inflation into general public benefit. A different President and Congress in circumstances like those of 1969 and 1970 could have combined monetary restriction, controls over prices and incomes, and higher taxes to reduce the inflationary temperature with funding out of new taxes for one or two million additional jobs in schools, hospitals, museums, parks, and law-enforcement agencies.

This is only to reiterate the truism that the manner in which a community approaches the problem of inflation is a sure indicator of its hierarchy of values. Galbraithians, as the foregoing suggests, are prone to treat recession as a chance to do something about persistent distortions in the social balance between public and private activities. Free-marketeers, to whom government is suspect as both inefficient, unresponsive to consumer preferences, and in the end, threatening to political liberty, are likely to prefer income maintenance (on a scale modest enough to avoid damaging work incentives) to public-job creation.

A corollary of the conservative posture concerns the nature of work and work incentives. In some conservative circles the belief is strong that most jobs are unrewarding. People undertake them only because otherwise they do not collect income with which to lead the good life of private consumption. Full employment makes it exceedingly hard to fill society's less attractive slots. The implicit virtue of recession is the pressure it exerts upon the unskilled and uneducated to wash cars, dishes, and laundry, collect the garbage of the affluent, work as domestics in their homes, and otherwise serve without complaint as hewers of wood and drawers of water. In a moment of candor Senator Russell Long complained about the Family Assistance Plan, on the ground that in his native Louisiana nobody would be available to do his shirts once the benefits of the plan became available to the laundresses.

Implicitly, then, a political decision to support maximum employment is also a decision to redesign the jobs that most people do. In the context of permanent labor shortage, private and public employers would be challenged to reshape routine jobs in ways that increased the satisfactions of doing them. Jobs for paraprofessionals are not in the long run enough unless doctors' aides can become doctors' assistants and other career ladders are constructed. The Lordstown syndrome,* the tight white collar, the blue-collar blues, and similar catchwords are

---

*General Motors constructed its new Vega assembly plant in the middle of the cornfields which surround Lordstown, Ohio. Heavy lifting was done by robots. Pay scales were high, but the predominantly young workers hated their work, performed many acts of sabotage, and mounted a long, wildcat strike against the tedium and routine of the assembly line. As at Lordstown, so elsewhere.

signs of widespread alienation at the job. The complaint
is common that the old-fashioned work ethic is in decline. The observation perhaps ought more frequently to
be made that men and women in a decent community
really should not be devoted to many of the tasks they are
now asked to undertake.

4.

"It is better," alleged Keynes in the mid-1920s, "to
disappoint the rentier than to cause unemployment."
The inflations which generate jobs also erode the savings
of the thrifty, the claims of creditors, and the pension
benefits of the elderly. The creditors at least, being
richer, were, for Keynes, less deserving of public concern
than considerably poorer laboring men and women.
There was a further reason justifying Keynes's priorities.
Inflation benefits the more enterprising members of the
community, among them housing developers, land
speculators, industrialists happy to borrow valuable dollars and repay their debts in depreciated currency, home
buyers who anticipate both capital gains from resale of
their property and mortgage burdens which are a diminishing percentage of the rising value of land and struc-
tures, and stock-market investors eager to share the
gains to be derived from a bull market.

By contrast, deflation dampens business activity and
discourages assumption of new risks. Old debts become
more burdensome and new ones less desirable to contract. As prices fall, unsold inventories of merchandise
decline in value. For new investment the outlook dark-
ens. Economic growth stutters and stops. Creditors no
doubt rejoice, but unemployment spreads through the
economy. If progress and growth are brethren, then inflation stimulates and deflation discourages them.

For the commercially astute and financially resourceful, the hedges against inflation are numerous and in each period inventive. Real estate is a traditional path to riches, although it is always possible to make a mistake about the particular parcel of property one acquires. Parke-Bernet auction prices, not to linger on the gaudier activities of the Metropolitan Museum of Art, attest to the possibilities of fine painting and sculpture as protections against rising prices. Of course it helps to possess and exercise discriminating judgment. One may speculate in commodities new and old. Again, there are no sure things. Bulk purchasers of Scotch whiskey futures have in many instances been painfully alerted to the tendencies of some whiskies to drop in price even as others continue to rise. Some Scotches are better than other Scotches. In relatively short order, improvements in California Cabernet Sauvignons are likely to bring an end to the wild escalation in price of French Bordeaux and Burgundies. Some owners of extensive wine cellars will be left with excellent wine but diminishing prospects of capital gains. Those who have plunged on silver have bet, as commodity speculators must, that demand will continue strong and government policy be unaltered.

I have described the risks and opportunities open for the most part only to the affluent. In an inflationary period, must ordinary citizens either promptly spend their income as they receive it or suffer steady erosion of savings, future pensions, and the real value of life insurance?

Not necessarily. Only a modicum of ingenuity suffices to design protections for the usual victims of steady-state inflation which makes the condition tolerable. Consider the elderly, the largest of the groups afflicted by inflation. Most of them get along on social security benefits, private pensions, Medicare reimbursements, and modest savings. These are our parents and grandparents. Self-

interest powerfully reinforces the community's natural
filial sentiment. If, between them, the elderly and the
Social Security Administration do not tolerably maintain
pensioners, then who but their children will do so?

Such musings as these probably explain the degree of
protection already instituted. Congress has acted to tie
the level of future social security benefits to the movements of the consumer price index. Since these payments are by far the largest single source of funds for the
retired, the protection is significant. Moreover, although
in 1973 the President proposed limitations of Medicare
coverage and increases in the beneficiaries' share of hospital costs, it is unlikely that Congress will concur and
probable that the longer-run tendency is toward expanded rather than contracted medical coverage of the
elderly.

When the consumer price index in a single year rises
6 percent, a $100 deposit in a 5 percent savings account
is worth $99 twelve months after it has been deposited.
The real rate of interest "earned" is a minus one percent. Those who have large sums of money can do much
better. Canny souls with at least an extra $100,000 can
purchase a certificate of deposit (sold in units of that
minimum size) whose interest return fluctuates with
movements in other interest rates. During inflation, interest rates, when they are legally free to do so, rise both
because borrowers of all descriptions want more credit
and lenders surrender their money only at interest rates
which measure expected losses in the value of the dollar.
In the absence of central-banking intervention, market
rates of interest tend to discount anticipated inflation.

These aspects of financial organization imply that only
relatively simple adjustments are required to diminish
present inequities of treatment of large and small savers.
A recent presidential commission has in fact recommended that interest-rate ceilings be lifted on small

deposits in thrift institutions.* After such a change, savings banks and savings and loan associations could compete in ways more rewarding to their customers than the giving of trivial gifts of luggage, toasters, and transistor radios for additional deposits. As their interest rewards rose, depositors would save more and, incidentally, help dampen inflation.

A solicitous government has many other opportunities. It is, for example, a historic inequity that savings bonds, available in small denominations for mass purchase, have been losing propositions. The Treasury has fixed their returns well below those frequently available to institutional and wealthy private investors. In principle the remedies are not excessively complex. The United States government could market a bond whose return fluctuated with other interest rates. Or, it might offer a lump-sum bonus at redemption which took account of the inflation which had accumulated during the life of the bond. Again, the Treasury could break down its marketable debt into $50 and $100 denominations, purchasable at post offices and savings banks. Why should the wealthy continue to enjoy a monopoly of the means of getting still richer?

As far as home mortgages are concerned, an available model is English practice. In Great Britain, lenders contract with home buyers on the basis of variable rates. How much a borrower pays in a given period then depends upon what happens to the money market. The arrangement possesses as its prime virtue the removal of

---

*The original justification of the ceiling arose from concern over banking stability. If bankers were able to compete freely for deposits, they might offer rates of return that were too high for their own stability. Since the Federal Deposit Insurance Corporation protects accounts up to $20,000, there is no danger of loss to the vast majority of savers. Nor is it clear that bankers are rasher than other businessmen, who are rarely guilty of giving their merchandise away.

the gambles of present American practice. Right now the home purchaser who buys when mortgage rates are down and holds on to his property benefits from a subsidy from the lender, during periods of inflation. Lenders collect similar subsidies from borrowers who were unlucky enough to negotiate during peak interest periods. Variable mortgage rates diminish the wide fluctuations in the availability of money for mortgages which present customs make inevitable.

Those who depend substantially on private pensions or state and local government retirement benefits also can be helped. After the successful model of the Teachers' Insurance and Annuity Association, a variable annuity feature could be incorporated into future private pension plans. The managers of variable annuity funds can purchase, on behalf of their clients, judiciously selected common stocks as hedges against inflation, just as rich individuals routinely do. Existing plans whose real benefits are lower than anticipated because of inflation might be declared eligible for federal supplementation either through the social security system or by way of direct Treasury payment.

As Ralph Nader* and others have demonstrated in some detail, half the workers who anticipate private pensions will receive not a penny, and many others will garner benefits smaller than they had been led to expect. Firms go bankrupt. Funds are inadequately financed. Or workers quit their jobs, and weak or missing vesting provisions fail to protect their stake. Hit-or-miss supervision by public agencies of the way private pension funds are administered opens the door wide to fraud on the part of fund managers. Badly needed, therefore, is congressional action which sets performance criteria and

*See Ralph Nader and Kate Blackwell, *You and Your Pension* (New York: Grossman, 1973).

institutes proper supervision. Within the boundaries of such a statute, it would be sensible to incorporate an escalator clause as protection against inflation.

No economic policy is perfect. The objections to learning to live with inflation are substantial. Among economists, accelerationists argue that it is foolhardy to anticipate that the economy could possibly operate at a steady rate of inflation. The general realization that this was the objective of national policy would be enough to arouse inflationary expectations, encourage union negotiators to extract larger wage and benefit increases, lead to inventory accumulation as hedge against rising replacement costs, and thus convert stable inflation into runaway inflation.

No one can be entirely certain that this danger could be avoided, because no Western government has tried the experiment of accepting inflation as a matter of social agreement and bipartisan economic policy. Several of the protections which might be instituted should have the effect of reducing spending, encouraging saving, and moderating inflation, not only through freer fluctuation of savings-bank interest but also through wider sale of marketable Treasury bonds and greater protection against the erosion or disappearance of private pension benefits.

Although the United States is less dependent on foreign trade than England, West Germany, or Japan, the balance of payments and the relation of the dollar to other currencies cannot safely be ignored, particularly since the American situation has been deteriorating for some years. For a relatively long period the over-all balance of payments which registers the effects of capital and tourist movements has been in deficit. More recently Americans have been buying more merchandise from foreigners than American exporters have persuaded foreign importers to purchase in exchange.

According to some stories, Japanese factory workers begin the morning by a rendition of the company song. In our auto and appliance plants, it is said, the sullen workers commence the day by smoking a joint or turning on to some drug of their preference. No wonder, then, that Japanese and German as well as Hong Kong, Korean, and Italian appliances, cars, motorcycles, cameras, steel, shoes, and textiles flood American markets and crowd out the shoddier and uncompetitively priced merchandise spewed from American mills and factories.

Prudent buyers in the American folklore take care to lay their hands on cars made outside of holiday seasons, and major athletic playoffs. They avoid vehicles assembled on Mondays and Fridays. The ideal American car is put together between 10 A.M. and noon on Wednesday morning under the personal supervision of the plant manager.

It does further damage to the balance of payments that so many citizens prefer to spend their vacation dollars in Europe rather than in the national parks of the United States. The Europeans have more history per square mile than our raw, new country has per square state.

Traditional analysts of foreign trade take these facts as additional arguments in favor of restraining American inflation, lest the situation further deteriorate. A country's credibility in the eyes of other nations and the strength of its diplomacy are directly associated with the prestige and popularity of its currency. When Britannia long ago ruled the waves, the pound sterling reigned supreme in the currency markets of London, Zurich, Amsterdam, Paris, and New York. After World War II when the American writ ran without challenge around the globe, all the world cried for dollars. The Marshall Plan and the loan to England were indulgent gestures by a benign giant to economic dwarfs. Even Dr. Kissinger cannot compensate for a shaky currency which signifies to cynical and ill-meaning foreigners an equally shaky economy. So, if America is not to become a weak, helpless giant, inflation must firmly be put down, and seen by our trading partners, to be put down.

The picture, as I have drawn it, is much too lurid. The sources, to begin with, of American balance-of-payments deficits are more numerous and less simple than the asserted devotion of the Japanese proletariat to the work ethic and the decline of this emotion here in the United States. Similar stories, popular a decade ago, which featured German love of work, have been succeeded by new militance on the part of German unions and new signs of proletarian restlessness on the part of the Teutons. Up to now the Japanese "miracle" has been facilitated by shift of large numbers of tenant farmers, living in semifeudal circumstances, to factories organized according to similar hierarchial principles where their efforts are more productive. Japanese managers are running out of docile farm labor, and it is improbable that the children of the present workers will sing the company hymn with the sincere enthusiasm of their parents.

Besides, a substantial portion of the deficit derives from the expense of our dozens of overseas bases, the hundreds of thousands of servicemen and civilian workers who staff them, and the aid which is extended to bastions of the free world in Greece, South Korea, Taiwan, Spain, and Indochina. Détente with Russia ought to imply, if not in the Nixon Administration, then in its successor, substantial withdrawals of forces from Western Europe.

Nor, even on the least cheerful estimates, has this country lost all of its competitive advantages. IBM is first and the rest of the world second in computer technology. The American lead is substantial in other busi-

ness machines, and in some industrial equipment into
the bargain. American agriculture, a monument to enlightened government policy,* is the most efficient in the
world. A third of all Russians on the farm cannot feed
themselves and their city cousins. The one American in
fourteen who tills the soil manages to produce surpluses
annually large enough to relieve Indian famine and Russian grain shortages.

The energy shortage† explains another percentage of
the American trading deficit. The pressure upon energy
sources enables the producing countries to jack up their
prices to oil consumers quite aside from the success of
the oil consumers in controlling domestic inflation.

In these matters, emphasis upon the American price
pattern is misleading. What counts is the comparisons
with the Germans, Japanese, Canadians, and other trading rivals. Even with the return of inflation in the spring
of 1973, American price behavior is no worse than British, French, and German inflation. Of course situations
shift abruptly. With the hubris that economists should
avoid, the Council of Economic Advisers boasted at the
beginning of 1973 that "One of the most striking
changes has been in the attitude of the international
economic community toward the American inflation;
before August 1971 it was the major concern of foreign
observers and investors. By the end of 1972 the American anti-inflation policy had become the marvel of the
rest of the world." A mere month before a second dollar
devaluation, the learned economists added: "Largely be-

---

*Land-grant universities and county agents have for more than a century
steadily expanded the information available to farmers and improved the
quality of farm operation. This aspect of socialism (naturally never so labeled)
has been a great success.
†I prefer "shortage" to "crisis" because the decline in oil and gasoline stocks
has more to do with American monopoly and Middle Eastern producer cartels
than with actual energy deficits.

cause of this change the rest of the world is willing to hold increasing amounts of dollars."* Such are the perils of economic analysis under political constraints.

However embarrassing to the Administration prophets, these misadventures fail to demonstrate that American inflation has been more rapid than Japanese, German, English, or French inflation. More mundanely, it appears that the devaluation of December 1971, hailed by Mr. Nixon as only slightly less momentous than the birth of Jesus Christ and the landing of the astronauts on the moon, was after all too small. It left the dollar overvalued especially in relation to the yen.

And as usual, experts and politicians had lost track of the changes which had occurred in monetary markets. Although gold speculation flourishes, gold has lost its role as a monetary reserve. No important currency is now tied to gold either in value or quantity. Vast sums of assorted currencies are in the treasuries of multinational corporations and oil sheiks. The sums involved dwarf the reserves available to central banks. When, out of nationalistic stupidity, countries try to preserve the value of their currency, speculators (i.e., these same multinationals and oil sheiks) enjoy almost guaranteed profits. They only need do what they did in 1970, 1971, and 1972: sell increasing numbers of dollars for yen and marks (which are artificially cheap so long as the dollar is pegged higher than its market value) in the certainty that sooner or later American authorities will withdraw their support for the dollar, allow it to decline in relation to other major currencies, and allow the speculators to reacquire a much larger number of dollars with the yen and marks that they had originally purchased.

Why should the rich and wicked (the terms are synony-

*See *Economic Report of the President*, January 1973 (Washington: Superintendent of Documents), p. 63.

mous) flourish without taking any of the risks which their apologists are accustomed to identify as justifying their profits? No reason. All that is necessary is for the monetary authorities to institute a "clean float." Translated, the jargon identifies a readiness to allow dollars to exchange freely for other currencies without interference by the Federal Reserve or the Treasury.

Clean floats promise two benefits. Currency speculators, no longer certain of events and facing new possibilities of loss, will limit their operations. Much more important, trade deficits and surpluses will tend to correct themselves. An American trading deficit diminishes foreign demand for dollars, enlarges American needs for yen, marks, francs, lire, and sterling, and almost instantly cheapens dollars and makes currencies in greater demand go up. Cheap dollars, which allow foreigners to buy more American goods for the same quantity of their own currency, add to the inflationary pressures of demand upon American markets. Expensive marks and yen raise the price of foreign goods (and travel abroad) for Americans. Soon American exports rise and American imports decline.

As usual, there are drawbacks. The most noticeable is the contract complications inserted into foreign trade by currency uncertainties. Large traders have already learned how to cope with these difficulties, mostly through hedging. Smaller traders will learn.

A graver issue arises from the connection between a policy of permanent inflation and the commitment to rapid economic growth which it implies. As Leonard Ross and Peter Passell have recently argued,* the politics of a conservative imperial power allow for only one antipoverty program. This is high, steady, economic growth which affords full employment and diminishes poverty. As they point out, during the 1960s continuous

*See their *Retreat from Riches* (New York: Viking, 1973).

economic expansion raised more men and women above the poverty line than all the Great Society programs lumped together. If a steady dose of inflation is the only recipe for growth, and growth the only hope for the poor, then men of good will may opt for inflation—if they are convinced that the costs of inflation are really lower than those of slower economic growth. Full employment is equally attractive to liberals and conservatives, at least as public objectives.

Nevertheless, if American egocentricity is to be avoided, there are weighty anti-growth arguments. Traditional emphases on economic growth as guarantors of rising living standards and emollients of social strife have to be reconsidered in the light of environmental deterioration, population pressure, emergent food shortages, and monopolistic organization of energy markets.*

Future American development and that of other advanced industrial nations will need to take place within the context of much enhanced emphasis upon antipollution technology and shifts from energy-guzzling huge autos to thriftier smaller ones. In all likelihood, sterner measures will be necessary, among them rationing of private cars (is one car per family a catastrophic measure?), encouragement to public transportation, and increasing emphasis upon human services which consume little capital and inflict little environmental damage.

Priorities can be reconsidered in an atmosphere of mild and persistent inflation. As always, there is some

---

*I have elsewhere complained that national-income statisticians have contributed to current overemphasis upon growth by their exaggeration of annual growth in GNP. So long as the costs of growth are lumped together with the benefits it will appear that producing more cigarettes (and medical treatment for lung cancer), automobiles (and antipollution equipment), whiskey (and anti-drinking clinics), and so on, promotes economic welfare. See my "Poverty of Affluence," in *Commentary* (April 1970), and *National Income and the Public Welfare* (New York: Random House, 1972).

danger that if gentle inflation proves tolerable it will promote dangerous complacency about the longer-term difficulties of American social and economic arrangements. It is equally evident that full employment is in itself no solution to excessive concentrations of economic power, unacceptable maldistribution of income wealth, decaying large cities, lagging racial integration, alienation from work, and the assorted ailments, trivial and serious, which afflict the American giant.

5.

According to preference, rational policy can protect the victims of either recession or inflation. As reactions to persistent inflationary bias, both policies have their attractions. Nevertheless, it is incontestable that recession, however humanely its casualties are soothed, does involve business loss, disruption of investor plans, and despair on the stock exchanges. The major reservation which attends sustained inflation is the danger of its acceleration. No one admires runaway inflation. Antitrust policy is intellectually the most consistent of remedies. However, it is politically remote because liberals and conservatives tend to shrink (for different reasons) from the disruptions it requires.*

There is another conceivable inflation strategy, represented by the moderate, technological left whose prophet is Galbraith.† It is futile, according to Galbraith,

---

*Practical conservatives are either afraid to rock the boat or beholden to some of the entrenched interests most vulnerable to free market strategies. On the whole, liberals are not especially entranced by free-market models. They are accordingly unmilitant about antitrust crusades designed to create them.
†There are echoes in Galbraith's *New Industrial State* of Veblen's emphasis upon experts and in Berle and Means' classic judgments of the loss of stockholder influence to professional management.

to dally with antitrust. Ineffective during the last eighty-three years, the Sherman Act (and the other relevant statutes) offer the promise of equivalent impotence for the next eighty-three.

The condition is not entirely or even mainly caused by the political strength of big business and the political pliability of members of Congress and Presidents, though these are never facts to be ignored. The larger explanation is located in the role of the large corporation as dominant economic institution. Technical economies of scale in some instances mandate large size, but for the most part the virtues of large corporations are organizational rather than technological. Galbraith has put the case in these terms:

. . . mention has been made of machines and sophisticated technology. These require, in turn, heavy investment of capital. They are designed and guided by technically sophisticated men. They involve, also, a greatly increased elapse of time between any decision to produce and the emergence of a salable product.

From these changes come the need and the opportunity for the large business organization. It alone can deploy the requisite capital; it alone can mobilize the requisite skills. It can also do more. The large commitment of capital and organization well in advance of result requires that there be foresight and that all feasible steps be taken to insure that what is foreseen will transpire. It can hardly be doubted that General Motors will be better able to influence the world around it—the prices and wages at which it buys and the prices at which it sells—then a man in suits and cloaks.*

In the thrust of the corporation to control its market, the state is a useful ally. The Pentagon is the largest, sometimes the only customer of aerospace and electron-

*See *The New Industrial State* (Boston: Houghton Mifflin, 1967), p. 4.

ics firms. For the business community at large, Keynesian fiscal policy amounts to a guarantee of aggregate
demand ample enough to keep sales and profits high.
The corporate wing of business has become in ideology
Keynesian, well before Mr. Nixon, because at length corporate planners comprehended the usefulness of assured high levels of demand. The variant of Keynesian
doctrine embraced is naturally conservative. Businessmen urge fiscal stimulation in the shape of investment
tax credits and reduced rates of personal and corporate
income tax. They oppose redistributive taxation and social spending focused on the poor. And their support of
aggregate demand stimulation by the federal government is likely to falter, short of full employment, out of
concern for labor discipline and union wage pressure.

Nevertheless, the commercial Keynesianism in vogue
among such centers of intelligent business discussion as
the Committee on Economic Development and *Business
Week* leaves executives free to do their own thing. Their
own thing is of course better and better planning, rational control of the corporate environment. Here the
large corporation commands the resources and presents
the most interesting intellectual challenges to experts of
many magics—engineers, accountants, media specialists,
marketing analysts, industrial psychologists, computer
wizards, systems analysts, and inevitably, economists
and lawyers. Such is the membership of the technostructure,* which explains the market mastery exercised by
large corporations.

The size and virtuosity of these corporations protects
them in the manipulation of their customers from the
vicissitudes of old-fashioned price competition in atom-
istic markets. Large corporations exercise a wide range
of choice over the products they choose to peddle, the

---

*A term of Galbraithian coinage.

places where they do the peddling, and the prices they charge. The organizational and technological superiorities of the modern large corporation transcend ideology. In socialist societies, government ownership of productive and marketing facilities has been entirely consistent with the development of parallel roles for socialist experts and for similar domination by the organizations, however styled, in which they function.

Neither for Galbraith nor for the present writer does this vision of reality imply that the power of the large corporation is inevitably or even usually benign. The thrust of the technostructure toward growth and stability may or may not coincide with the public interest. Certainly, large corporations do not shape their plans according to even their own conception of public interest. Possibly, as Galbraith believes, in the long run the experts upon whom the giant enterprises rely will civilize corporate behavior. The experts and thus the corporation are susceptible to the influence of the Educational and Scientific Estate, headquartered in the universities from which they secured their professional credentials.* For the time being, however, it is not sensible to expect major corporations to spontaneously protect the environment, promote racial harmony, and contribute to improved public services while at the same time they maximize their own growth and market shares. It is equally delusory to anticipate that any time soon our corporate masters will substitute the pursuit of principle for the hunt for profit and encourage either competition or innovation.

And, as has already appeared, large corporations are faint-hearted warriors against inflation. They are subject

---

*Of course, there is the less attractive probability that the corporations will transform the universities in their own image, rather than the other way around.

to frequent weaknesses for higher prices and smaller sales in preference to a reversal of the adjectives. They can and do enlist their international connections to limit the efficacy of domestic monetary restraints. Often their supranational status allows them to evade domestic regulation.

If these Wilt Chamberlains of finance and industry are (as they appear to be) here to stay, and if, as is equally true, they exercise power which is both politically illegitimate* and practically undersupervised by public authority, then the general implication is self-evident: against private power must be arrayed still stronger (and more legitimate) public power.

Permanent controls properly center upon institutions which exert permanent private power. It follows that the candidates for public attention extend beyond the major corporations to national trade unions, life insurance giants, professional societies, and health intermediaries like Blue Cross and Blue Shield. The appropriate condition of eligibility for supervision is an affirmative answer to the question, Does the candidate, corporate or other, significantly influence the world in which he operates? Are prices, market shares, rate of innovation, wages, fees, entry into industry, craft, or profession subject to the decisions of an identifiable group of people?

No one is a good judge of his own cause. In every circumstance human beings tend to prefer their own to the general interest. Among them doctors, hospitals, and private insurers have collected some billions of dollars of Medicare and Medicaid funds while supplying remarkably few additional health services. Local bar associations routinely circulate minimum-fee schedules apply-

---

*The voters did not elect Harold Geneen Secretary of State or director of the Central Intelligence Agency. Nor did they select Henry Ford II as the arbiter of British labor relations.

ing to the drawing of wills and contracts, property clos-
ings, and divorce court representation, so as to avoid
"unethical" price competition among the brethren.* At
the same time, lawyers quietly collect rebates from title
insurers, without confiding in their clients. Although it is
to its credit that the national AFL-CIO has consistently
supported civil rights statutes, individual construction
locals continue systematically to exclude blacks and
members of other minorities,† until Congress belatedly
stirred.

In these and similar instances, restrictive practice
raises the price of product or service. Because the number of construction workers is limited, their hourly rates
are higher and fewer houses are built. If the lawyers
applied the antitrust rules to their own activities, more
litigants could afford better legal representation. Health
costs would rise less aggravatingly if the relationship of
doctors, hospitals, and insurers were less affectionate.

As we have seen, market power in time of recession
implies the ability to resist for months or years reductions in wages, prices, and which is the "normal" response to shrinking demand. Although in the end these
adjustments are made, the delay is painful and the recession longer because market power protects its posses-
sors against the full blast of economic adversity.

Before proceeding to consideration of the controls
that are needed, we should reassert a distinction between cost-push and demand-pull inflation. At any moment the two varieties are likely to be interwoven. In the

*The convention in such matters appears to be that customs which raise
professional income are ethical and those which lower client costs are unethical.
†According to the usual "defense," unions discriminate on a virtually universal basis against every applicant except a child of a present member—without
regard to race, religion, or national origin.

spring of 1973, for instance, food prices soared even more rapidly than other prices because the customers tried to buy more meat and groceries than farmers and processors could supply (at prices then current). Accordingly, prices rose until supply and demand were again equal. This is to say, people bought less or worse food. Such is demand-pull inflation. Also present were cost-push elements provided by the crop limitations and price supports administered by the Department of Agriculture and by the political decision in 1972 to sell massive quantities of wheat to the Russians.

The general remedy for demand-pull inflation centers on the federal budget. Taxes must rise, federal spending decline, or both. As matters of fiscal hydraulics there is little to choose between tax and expenditure policy so long as a sufficient number of dollars are by either device removed from the control of consumers and businessmen who otherwise, by spending them, would add to inflationary demand.

The social consequences of fiscal policy flow from the identity of those who pay higher or lower taxes, and the manner in which tax receipts are redirected. Tax changes can be egalitarian, inegalitarian, or neutral in their impact upon the distribution of income and wealth. The gainers from larger Pentagon appropriations are different from the beneficiaries of more money for public housing and public-job creation. In the end, politics are likely to dictate the composition of either fiscal stimulus or fiscal sedation. Save in comparatively rare circumstances, Congress is readier to cut taxes than raise social spending. At least in recent years the lawmakers also prefer to reduce social programs in boom times rather than raise taxes on individuals and corporations.

A second preliminary point ought to be disposed of. As free-market economists have accurately asserted, incomes policies have, since 1945, been applied to prices, wages, rents, and profits in England, Scandinavia, the Low Countries, and elsewhere. In the end, as Chicago economists joyfully report, control arrangements everywhere break down upon the rocks of instransigent corporate and union resistance. This historical generalization, rather inconvenient to partisans of controls, is understandably taken to demonstrate that politicians who interfere with market processes waste their time and effort unless they are prepared to finally substitute central state direction for the jostling of free markets.

Aspirant controllers need not meekly surrender their aspirations. For it is also historically true that none of the countries whose incomes policies initially succeeded and subsequently collapsed has been able to avoid renewed experiment. A convenient example is England. During Harold Wilson's term in office, 1964–1970, the Labour government tried not very successfully several varieties of price and income control. Much after the fashion of Nixon economic policy, the Labour ministers managed to increase unemployment without very dramatically reducing the pace of inflation.

Drawing the seemingly appropriate political inference, Edward Heath, whose ideological preferences approximated those of early Richard Nixon, pledged himself and all right-thinking Tories to economic freedom: no controls, no concessions to the trade unions, and no succor for failing British corporations. This "dash to freedom" was expected to tone up flabby managerial muscles, weaken the tyranny of trade unions, and in short order restore Britain to a distinguished place in the world trading community.

It sounded fine. Yet, within a year Mr. Heath was busily engaged in rescuing Rolls Royce and the Upper Clyde Shipyards from bankruptcy. Within another year, he was to be seen copying American Phase I and Phase II controls. By 1973, it was difficult to distinguish Tory freedom from socialist planning. Mr. Heath had even dragged through Parliament (over vehement Labour opposition) an Industrial Relations Act which embarrassingly resembled a measure proposed (and then withdrawn) by the Labour government.

Such events need not be startling. In the United States as in England, and no doubt elsewhere in democratic communities, no major party, whether it calls itself liberal, conservative, or socialist, is able (or willing) to break up the major corporations or unions to which the politicians are beholden for cash contributions and other support. In its present inhumanitarian guise, planned recession is politically dangerous and slow to operate. Thus far no government has seemed inclined to proclaim inflation as a permanent and potentially tolerable condition. Since the voters punish officeholders for the serious discomforts of inflation and unemployment, it behooves Presidents and prime ministers somehow to moderate the first without exacerbating the second. Not of course the easiest of political recipes.

However they begin, the political chefs soon learn that fiscal and monetary ingredients are not enough. They stir into the political mixture some kind of controls. Perhaps it is in the nature of late capitalism that the controls are both essential and exceedingly difficult to formulate so as to please the major economic actors.

The controllers have been most successful on the occasions when popular wars have aroused patriotism and stimulated a sense of common purpose. However extensive the control apparatus may be, it fails without voluntary public compliance. Willingness to comply in turn comes from general perception of equity in the way the control system is operated.

As recent American history implies, controls can work during a withdrawal from an unpopular war to a precarious peace. In 1971 the wage-price freeze and the detailed controls of Phase II enjoyed public support because the veneer of equity was uncracked. A total freeze is an event, at least under 1971 conditions, so totally unanticipated that neither the business nor the labor players have a chance to profit by advance warning. As in the children's game, the rule governs that soon the music will resume and the competitors again tensely circle the chairs.

Phase II was predictably more complicated. The wage guidepost was more specific than the profit-margin restraints which accompanied it. Landlords and dividend recipients were subject to still vaguer rules. Although the rules failed to please all who were subject to them, and their application aroused occasional yelps of pain, unions and corporate managers refrained from open rebellions. Indeed the sharp stock-market break after Phase II controls were removed on January 11, 1973, and the renewed speculation against the dollar suggest that businessmen and investors had learned to coexist comfortably with controls.

It is safe to predict that whatever the twists and turns of Administration policy during President Nixon's second term of office, controls of some kind over some prices and some incomes will repeatedly be necessary.

It is then wise to examine the characteristics of an equitable control system. It begins with appropriate statutory authority. The Kennedy-Johnson guidelines relied on nothing more substantial than discussions in the *Economic Reports of the President,* press conference statements, and occasional applications of presidential muscle.* The Economic Stabilization Act, under which

---

*Not that these were invariably ineffective. As President Kennedy proved in his April 1962 confrontation with U.S. Steel's Roger Blough, the Chief Executive of the United States can make the chief executive of U.S. Steel back down even without statutory backing if he is willing to threaten diversion of defense contracts, grand jury inquiries into possible antitrust violations, and Internal Revenue Service investigations of corporate financial affairs.

President Nixon acted in August 1971, was an extremely vague and general grant of authority to the President. It was generally understood as a ploy by congressional Democrats to embarrass a Republican President who was never expected to exercise his unsought powers.

Since then, Congress has twice renewed the act with minor modifications. The more recent version, that of April 30, 1973, broadens the exemption from wage restraints of low-income workers. All the same, the pretense is general that the statute and the powers it grants to the Chief Executive are temporary. Normal "freedom" of economic action, according to the congressional pieties, is at hand.*

In the long run, credible controls require durable congressional endorsement. The condition demands that some Congress and President suspend this mutual search of political advantage long enough to negotiate and agree on the design, passage, and presidential acceptance of a permanent control statute which establishes a constitutional framework for incomes policy.

Permanence is the easiest of qualities to specify, if not necessarily to attain. Harder requirements are appropriate administrative machinery and equitable standards of procedure. In World War II the War Labor Board was tripartite—labor, management, and public. In 1971 and 1972 the Phase II Pay Board copied this model but was in short order boycotted by most labor members. That the machinery did not collapse as a result may imply that what is essential is less explicit membership on control agencies by major interests than assurance that control authorities will deal fairly with all the economic players.

*A personal instance. A member of the House Banking Committee asked the present writer and two other economists testifying on control renewal in March 1973 to inform him when controls could be eliminated and free markets "restored." Such are the yearnings of many congressmen and senators.

The machinery is important, and the quality of those who control it is vital. But the heart of incomes policy is equity. Permanent supervision of incomes and prices compels someone somewhere to decide if not what is equity in payment, then what is equity in changing the rewards drawn from assorted economic activities. These rewards are distributed in strange and wondrous fashion. Frank Hogan, who became district attorney of Manhattan before most of the borough's residents were born, draws an official salary of $39,000. Frank Field, weatherman for a local television channel, gets $70,000 for communicating with charm the daily forecasts of the United States Meteorological Service, while CBS confers $250,000 on Walter Cronkite. Chase Manhattan chairman, David Rockefeller pulls down $230,000 and no doubt pieces out his stipend with other sources of income, but his brother Nelson, New York State's eternal governor, makes do with $85,000 for supervising the affairs of twenty million residents. As proprietor of New York's Liberal party, Alex Rose takes only $18,-200, none of it from Liberals, and all of it for his services as president of the United Hatters, Cap and Millinery Workers. As captain and center of the World Champion New York Knickerbockers, Willis Reed enjoys a more attractive $250,000 plus income from endorsements. Different people get very different results from running various things. For $50,000 John V. Lindsay more or less manages New York City, and for the same sum Albert Shanker unmistakably directs the United Federation of Teachers. Richard Nixon handles the country for $200,000, and Harold Geneen the equally tangled affairs of ITT for $812,311. The City University pays the distinguished political scientist Hans Morgenthau $31,000, and a local radio station the distinguished disk jockey Don Imus a round $200,000. New York City's deputy mayor gets $45,000, and Hugh M. Hefner of *Playboy* fame $317,000.*

Would anyone of sound mind, politically right, left, or center, design a system of compensation which featured such outcomes? Not likely. In whose sight is the host of a radio talk show six times as valuable as the mayor of the nation's biggest city, and ten times worthier than an academic star? Economists are not baffled by this sort of persiflage. What free markets create, they do not question. Well-trained social scientists refrain from value judgments about the comparative merits of Boone's Apple Farm Wine and Beaulieu Vineyards Cabernet Sauvignon (Special Reserve) 1968; *Playboy* and the *American Economic Review; Last Tango in Paris* and *The Sorrow and the Pity;* chess and professional basketball; scientists and salesmen; consumers' advocates and advertising pitchmen; and so on and on. All that need be said, or nearly all, is this: the talk-show host deserves his $300,000 for the simple and sufficient reason that large numbers of people out there like his show well enough to turn their sets on and hearken to the messages of advertisers who buy time. Presumably, if the electorate were convinced that $300,000 would hire a President 50 percent more competent or 75 percent less deceptive, they would urge Congress to make the appropriate pay adjustment.

In the purest of market arguments, the Latin motto holds: *de gustibus non est disputandum.* If there is no merit in arguing about tastes, there is no use complaining about the rewards different people who gratify these tastes receive from the economic system. We daily set out and daily alter the rules by the manner in which we spend money and select political representatives. As public preferences shift, so shortly does the point on the

*See *New York,* May 7, 1973, pp. 42–48, for these and a great many more income revelations.

income scale at which a person comes momentarily to rest. Assuming financial probity, a man of talent might enjoy the power and prestige of office more than an income several times as large as his public salary. If he is satisfied, who is to say him nay or to quibble about the relative modesty of his earnings?

Before we allow ourselves to be carried away by the austere beauties of the theory, it might be well to recall that the theory holds only when markets are competitive and customers are uncoerced. Only then* can it plausibly be argued that individual financial rewards mirror economic merit. But the tastes of the customers are surely altered by advertising, else why do the advertisers bother? And, as has repeatedly emerged in our account, wherever unions, corporations, universities,† and professional societies have interposed tollgates, the returns of the monopolists are higher than those to be derived from a truly free market.

Prejudice also distorts income. Until a generation ago white baseball players earned far more than black players of equal merit because until the late Jackie Robinson, big-league baseball was a segregated sport. Despite improvement attributable to the civil rights movement of the 1960s, Women's Liberation, civil rights statutes, and affirmative action programs in corporations and universities, color and sexual prejudice continue to generate lower incomes for women and blacks than for white males of comparable qualifications. And although progress has been substantial, it is still disadvantageous in

---

*But inheritance is an embarrassment even here. What can be said of a large income from inherited property which mirrors the merit of the donor, not the heir?

†Whatever its general merit, tenure for university teachers raises average academic salaries, frustrates the entry of younger scholars, raises the cost of university education, and presumably restricts the number of young people who can afford higher education.

some income contexts to be Jewish, Italian, Polish, or even plain Roman Catholic.

Government decisions influence or determine a great many individual incomes. Some are transfers, such as social security, veterans' benefits, and welfare, but others include subsidies to farmers, shipbuilders, oil companies, defense contractors, and a long list of others. As interpreted in the Internal Revenue Code, congressional tax policies create by some estimates anywhere from $65 to $75 billion of income otherwise eligible for the attention of the Internal Revenue Service collectors.

The tax system is a noble source of inequity. Average souls of average income earn wages and salaries on which taxes are scrupulously withheld by their employers. The merely affluent and the really wealthy benefit from indulgent tax treatment of capital gains, returns from oil properties, tax-exempt municipal bonds, business-expense deductions, and estate-tax exemptions. In the eyes of the tax collector, it is far more forgivable to report $100,000 in capital gains than the same sum as salary. The gaudy plumage of the Texas multimillionaire in his native habitat noisily testifies to the power of tax law to enrich.

Then there is inheritance. Is an heir entitled to credit for prudent selection of his parents? According to what market criteria does a little Rockefeller or an infant Ford merit income from the trusts established in his name? Economists have either skated uneasily around this issue or, alternatively, argued that unless inheritance is protected, incentive to work and accumulate will be fatally injured. Will it? Do the rich take risks (which incidentally benefit the community) in order to achieve vicarious immortality in the persons of their children and grandchildren? Or is it the lure of the game and the urge to outdo rivals which are at work? A way to discover the truth of the matter is to impose heavy taxes on large estates. Short of this innovation, we shall continue to live with the anomaly of a market economy which supports large numbers of persons on income that their own market contributions do not justify.

The upshot is a judgment that existing inequalities of income, which concentrate nearly 30 percent in the most fortunate top tenth and allot a meager 3.7 percent to the bottom *fifth,* are far from entirely the work of competition. At work as well are inheritance, monopoly, prejudice, tax favoritism, public subsidies, welfare policies, and many other allocative influences. Large incomes and small incomes *may* approximate the relative economic contributions of those who receive them. Nothing makes this outcome a certainty.

Historically, Americans have been amazingly tolerant of the rich, unenvious of inherited affluence, and disposed to admire their large corporations. Rich politicians frequently fare well in elections, possibly because their supporters hope they will not find it necessary to steal the state treasury. The corporations appear to have convinced at least some of their customers that they are veritable paragons of competition. In American politics, economic growth has usually substituted for divisive discussion of income redistribution. If the pie swells every year, even the small pieces get bigger.

This amiable consensus is upset by emergencies which require manifest government intervention. During large-scale war, it offends natural justice to allow a few to enrich themselves while others risk their lives at most and their comforts at least. It is easy during such a time to impose excess-profits taxes, raise levies on personal and corporate income, shame people into buying more war bonds than they really want, and ration scarce items of food, clothing, and gasoline. It is not fair to let the rich eat all the steak. Even the rich are inclined to agree.

Inflations are less unifying than popular wars. Corporations and unions enroll American citizens, not storm troopers and kamikazi pilots. Here precisely is the crux of the controllers' dilemma. In the abstract the choice is between accepting present income outcomes and keeping the shares of the different interests constant or, nudging the control system, in the direction of equity, however that elusive word is politically defined.

Phase II controls, as in a conservative Administration might have been expected, adhered to the first criterion. The 5.5 percent wage guideline was derived by adding an allowance for anticipated inflation (2.5 percent) to an estimated productivity-improvement figure (3 percent). Profit margins were to follow the experience of the preceding three years. No one was supposed to expand his share at the expense of others. The 1971 division of the economy's loot between wages and profits was taken as the standard for 1972's wage and price performance.

When the President abruptly terminated controls, he left the crucial issues in abeyance. If Phase II controls had been retained, how would they have operated during a period of incipient profit inflation? By the beginning of 1973, increasing numbers of corporations were in a position, the controls permitting, to raise their prices high enough to earn profits well in excess of the margin limitations of the Price Commission. What would the Price Commission have done to enforce its own rules? Would corporations have obeyed rules which cost them increasing sums of money?

During a boom, profits rise more rapidly than other income shares. When controls linger into a boom, they focus general uneasiness about the equity of arrangements which allow businessmen and stockholders to collect a lion's share of the fruits of expansion but impose the brunt of the pains of recession upon small businessmen and groups particularly vulnerable to unemployment—blacks, Chicanos, women, and youths.

Property gains from expansion and working people lose from contraction. The asymmetry is flagrant enough to arouse even an occasional leader of a construction union. The language of Edward J. Carlough, head of the Sheet Metal Workers International Association, echoes a strain of traditional populism:

The working people of this country are being swindled down to their socks by a political Administration that's either too ignorant to understand or just doesn't give a damn. . . . the biggest 880 companies in the United States last year made profits—after taxes—of $52.6 billion, an all-time record. This was in a year when the guy in overalls had his wages frozen part of the year, and controlled the rest of the year. . . . We so-called great and powerful American trade unionists have become a tray of cream puffs. We're being gouged by the price fixers and clobbered by the tax collectors, while all the time our unemployment rate continues at over 5 per cent nationally, and over 10 per cent for construction workers. We're so puffed up and polite with our middle-class status—we great "silent majority" —that the jackals are eating us alive.*

This is the sort of reaction which compels wage and price controllers, however conservative their original stance, to rectify or at least appear to rectify the more glaring injustices of control arrangements. It is also one of the reasons why in all mixed, capitalist economies, controls break down. The number of special cases increases. Unions cry foul. Corporations which for the first time in years scent profit are hampered by profit-margin controls that condemn them to the criteria of years in which they were doing poorly. By contrast, corporations which were faring well during the base period are encouraged to do still better.

During Phase II, special cases were fairly numerous.

*See the *New York Times* (May 3, 1973), p. 43.

Reflecting either the equities or the politics of each situation, the Pay Board approved a West Coast longshoremen's contract much beyond the 5.5 percent standard on the ground that unusual improvements in worker productivity were guaranteed by the agreement. A still earlier Pay Board exercise involved teachers in public schools whose increases initially were frozen and eventually released. Here the peculiarities of the academic calendar, the pay practices of school boards, and the fact that the increases had been negotiated (though not paid to the teachers) before Phase I, rationalized special treatment.

Though its proceedings were considerably less public than those of the Pay Board, the Price Commission also identified many candidates for price increases in excess of stated standards. Some students of the two agencies have tentatively concluded that the Pay Board was rather more effective in the limitation of higher wages than the Price Commission was in holding down prices and profits.*

Intuition and common observation buttress econometric analysis. After all, wage contracts are highly visible, and employers share the aspirations of the controllers to check "excessive" increases. Unions, on the other hand, have less reason to police their employers' prices because they spend little or none of their income on a given employer's products. The actual situation is often even more hostile to strong price control, for unions may be perfectly willing to allow companies to raise prices if this is the easiest way to get more money for themselves. Prices, moreover, can quietly be raised by lowering quality or, as in packaged foods, reducing quantities. When

---

*See, for example, "Phase II: The U.S. Experiment with an Incomes Policy," by Barry Bosworth, in *Brookings Papers on Economic Activity*, 2 (1972), pp. 343–84.

a large company markets a great many different items, even keeping track of its prices is a job for the experts. Most of the experts work either for the corporations or the controllers rather than for unions or truly independent organizations.

The retreat of the Nixon Administration in 1973 from effective controls was an escape from the dilemmas of equity. Bad luck, politics, and poor management of agricultural policy raised food prices at sickening rates to sickening new highs. Major corporations celebrated Phase III with a burst of price hikes. The oil companies and the media promulgated the news of an energy crisis. By the beginning of May the cost of living was going up 9 percent a year; the GNP deflator, a more sluggish index, was rising at a 6 percent rate; and consumers were flocking to the stores in a storm of preventive buying before the new and higher prices they gloomily anticipated. If the customers failed to calm down, they would spend 16 percent more in 1973 than in 1972.

Equity now demanded of a pro-business, anti-control Administration a whole series of uncomfortable actions. To check the demand-pull component of inflation, the best response was a sizable tax surcharge on personal and corporate income and the suspension of the investment tax credit. Dealing with a Democratic Congress, the White House would probably have to accept, as the political price of congressional approval, heavier burdens on corporations and affluent individuals than on ordinary earners.

Some of the inflationary pressure was cost-push in origin. Where corporations had pushed prices too high, the indicated response is partial or complete rollback to final Phase II levels. Controls would have to apply to farmers as well as food processors if there was to be a hope of checking further escalation of the consumer price index.

Only after such steps as these could the White House credibly ask unions to adhere to moderation in contract demands and ultimate settlements. Unions, as Mr. Carlough's pungent words attest, are outraged at huge profits unaccompanied by huge wage improvements. Union negotiations will necessarily seek the second if nothing is done about the first.

Thus, at the start of 1973 the President was confronted with an unpleasant choice. To really restrain inflation required him to seek tax increases certain to inflict financial injury on generous contributors to the Committee for the Re-election of the President. Equitable price rollbacks injured large corporations still more. Effective controls on food were sure occasions for outrage down on the farm. The matter would be still graver if food and gasoline rationing became inevitable supplements to price and wage controls. It is not an exaggeration to conclude that an effective program was certain to offend most of the members of President Nixon's election coalition. And since it is very difficult, if not impossible, to disappoint the expectations of businessmen without depressing stock prices and reducing real investment, a genuine assault upon inflation practically guaranteed an early recession.

What to do? A way to escape the sharp pangs of choice between efficacious policy and political expense is the very course chosen by the President in January: let the economy go and hope that inflation will of its own accord simmer down before still another policy reversal compels a Phase IV freeze followed by Phase V wage-price controls. Here, then, is an almost classic example of why controls break down: they become politically too costly to be borne by Presidents and prime ministers.

Is it really possible to tame the strong in a capitalistic society? On the evidence, an affirmative answer is not easy to give.

IV.
Conclusion

Economists know *how* to control inflation.

The interesting issues center upon the ethical and political limitations upon the deployment of reliable weapons of fiscal, monetary, and price-wage policies. How much can the economists do when so many of the more prominent economic actors influence or control their own fate? How powerful is economic rationality against the self-interest and political influence of giant corporations?

Inflation flourishes in a culture of inequality, for it feeds upon envy and the comparisons which plutocracy almost daily compels everyone to make. A case in point stars New York City's firemen. Here is a job which demands physical agility and physical courage. Few begrudge firemen decent pay and parity with police salaries, the present New York arrangement. Never knowing when one's own life and property may rest upon prompt response from the nearest fire company, New Yorkers want their protectors to be content.

Alas, they are not. In the spring of 1973 the incumbent firemen's union president lost to a challenger who stressed as a campaign issue the unacceptable narrowing of the "traditional" gap between firemen and sanitation workers. Apparently the fact that fire fighters and policemen were doing remarkably well was less important than the loss of face involved in the even larger gains of an "inferior" group.

When labor is a commodity and most jobs are disheartening to the instinct of workmanship, status is likely to be tied to relative income. Accordingly, disturbances in "historic" relationships affront those on next higher rungs of status ladders. The school board that grants elementary teachers parity with their high school colleagues practically guarantees indignant attempts by the latter to regain traditional differentials. Gains by the carpenters are sufficient occasion for gains by the electricians. Steelworkers must do at least as well as auto workers. Within the federal bureaucracy, payment according to comparable private-sector rates spreads wage inflation from the private to the public sector. Major law firms set flagrantly high starting salaries for new associates fresh out of Yale or Harvard Law School,* as much to advertise their own leadership over lesser law factories as to measure immediate contribution from legal neophytes.

The salaries of corporate executives are counters in a status race at the highest level, no different in quality from the behavior of jealous unions and lawyers and the anxieties which afflict other entrants in other rat races.

Inflation jars the conventional structure of comparison and in turn is stimulated by the reflexive efforts of workers, managers, and professional workers to reassert their "just" position. Matters are worsened when the

---

*Starting salaries in major Wall Street firms are edging up to $20,000. Is a recent graduate worth more than a veteran patrolman? If it has not already done so, the question is likely to occur to the Patrolmen's Benevolent Association.

contenders try to improve their relative position, for unless those just above amiably accept the change, they will shortly be out on the barricades fighting for justice.

As an ailment of status insecurity in a society which conventionally associates wealth with merit, inflation is stimulated by the visibility of wide disparities of economic reward. Egalitarians would narrow these disparities by progressive income taxation and heavy inheritance levies. Anti-egalitarians, a sizable majority by the indicator of the 1972 election, prefer to take their chances of fortune in the hope that they or their children will make it big. An interesting feature of the McGovern campaign was the degree to which men and women of moderate resources felt threatened by proposals that were intended to improve their own situation—but do still more for poorer people. Senator McGovern's income redistribution plan, however clumsily presented, did promise to shift substantial sums from the richest third of the population to the remainder. A naïve soul could have expected the demogrant to be wildly popular with two out of every three voters and opposed by the third.

Yet, save for a few equality freaks, the demogrant was the occasion of almost universal distaste. The explanations usually advanced are two. One was the suspicion that dropouts from the work ethic—hippies and undeserving welfare families—were to be the major gainers. Improvement in their status was readily interpreted as parallel deterioration in the reputation of respectable blue- and white-collar types. Possibly also, the $12,000 breaking point between recipients and suppliers of benefits offended those earning $10,000 or $11,000 and expecting soon to increase their income well above the magic McGovern number. One can only guess which of these prospects was more repulsive—gifts to the unworthy or taxes on the worthy to pay for them.

Inflation is a problem of the heart. What a society does about it depends upon the quality of human mercy and the bonds of sympathy which bind members of a community to each other. Within the limits of market capitalism, each of the four approaches which has occupied our attention implies a different conception of the pains that legitimately can be inflicted on some members of society, and of the protections that equity requires for those injured in the general interest. In Western Europe and the United States, the complexity and inconsistency of anti-inflation policy since World War II are the direct consequence of shifting perceptions of the socially acceptable in economic action, by governments and others.

The choice among free markets, deliberate recession, livable inflation, and permanent controls defines the character of an operating economy. Consistent application of free-market principle requires radical restructuring of large corporations, unions, and the government agencies which now confront them. More than that, each social arrangement—public schools, professional accreditation, public welfare, and government subsidies of any kind—must be re-examined as a possible barrier to free competition. Unfettered markets epitomize what Irving Kristol has praised as "thinking economically" and what he has associated, like Friedrich Hayek and Milton Friedman before him, with the preservation of political liberty.* In the eyes of Kristol and his teachers, the purely economic benefits of competition include less-

---

*In "Capitalism, Socialism, and Nihilism," *The Public Interest* (Spring 1973). The Chicago School of Economics has for three generations argued two major propositions. The first is a claim that free choice for consumers and efficiency on the part of producers require genuine price competition among many relatively small sellers. The second is the judgment that as competition is eroded, government becomes more powerful and societies slide downhill toward, in Friedrich Hayek's famous book title, *The Road to Serfdom.* Why the Chicago School is not in the vanguard of antitrust is one of the minor intellectual mysteries of our time.

ened susceptibility to inflation and greater pressure for efficiency. Just as the rewards of the efficient are alluring, the penalties of the inefficient are swift and salutary—financial ruin.

The social corollaries are substantial. Since competitive drives are to be stimulated, the social services and cash benefits offered to laggards in the competitive races must necessarily be so modest that altruism never sabotages the impetus to help oneself by individual striving. Thus Milton Friedman's original negative-income-tax scheme* recommended elimination of existing social service programs and cash payments to the poor pegged no higher than 50 percent of the 1962 poverty level—$1,500 each year for families of four members. Not only would the poor get too little to discourage search for gainful employment, they would be granted freedom to spend as they chose the small sums that came their way. It is standard free-market ideology that individuals are the best judge of their own welfare.

The values glorified by the economic way of thought are those of self-reliance, rational calculation, and competitive struggle. Freedom of choice, as well as efficiency and growth, are among the benefits. The penalties include encouragement of aggression and avarice (never in short supply) and discouragement of altruism, whether individual or corporate.

Although it is possible to imagine "equitable" recessions in which the victims of national policy are compensated in cash or employment, the costs of the kind of recession that we typically have are substantial. Those who have administered them have usually been less concerned with the fate of the unemployed or bankrupt than with priority of stopping inflation. In the hierarchy of

*See his *Capitalism and Freedom* (Chicago: University of Chicago Press, 1962).

values revealed by action, inflation is worse than unemployment, creditors deserve protection more than debtors do, and a sound balance of international payments is worthier of admiration than even wholesome rates of economic growth.

Deliberate recession can dampen inflationary expectations, cool investment booms, and compel unions to moderate their demands. In the United States, the great modern experiment occurred during the 1950s when three recessions, sluggish growth, and high unemployment did in the end destroy the inflationary psychology fed by the Korean War. The policy took a long time, and inflicted a great deal of hardship. It served very clearly to reveal the capacity of entrenched market power to resist fiscal and monetary pressure.

A probable lesson of the Nixon years is that this President's shakier grip on the affections of his countrymen made it impossible to repeat the policies of the 1950s. They would take still longer to work themselves out because corporate concentration has increased and because the greater prominence of multinational operation has expanded opportunities to evade domestic economic restraints.

At least in a conservative climate, planned recession is socially the most reactionary of responses to inflation. It is the strategy above all others most certain to enlarge unemployment among racially, demographically, and sexually vulnerable groups. Recession pushes increasing numbers of the just-barely-not-poor below the poverty line. The fears and anxieties over personal security generated by recession impede social reform, tighten labor discipline, promote humility on the campuses, and increase the power of bankers and other creditors.

Implicit in affection for recession as anti-inflation therapy is a conception of human nature closer to Hobbes than Rousseau: men and women will do the tedious work of the world, and heed their employers' necessarily oppressive regulations, only as they are pricked by the spur of fear—of job and income loss. The drives against welfare loafers which are popular political sports during recessions are warnings to more respectable members of the working poor that there are fates worse than dull and ill-paid jobs.

Recession postpones improvement of working conditions, still cries, genuine as well as modish, of work alienation, and preserves the comforts of the prosperous. Household help becomes plentiful and grateful. No shirt need remain unlaundered.

Each remaining strategy contains its own social valuations. To live with inflation and make it tolerable for its usual victims argues less that inflation is a good thing than that most Americans are averse to significant structural change of either the free market or redistributionist varieties. An imperial power like the United States, particularly during one of its conservative moods, is unlikely to favor cash transfers to the poor, an expanded public sector, guaranteed government employment, or incitement of the politically passive urban proletariat by community-action devices. However, the work ethic is endorsed rather than affronted by high employment essentially in the private sector. Hence full employment becomes the only politically viable antipoverty strategy. Inflation is to be borne in the interests of full employment. It is to be expected because the inflationary tilt to the American economy is permanent. Growth is better than recession because unemployment is far worse than inflation.

Finally, the case for controlling the strong starts from several assumptions about the modern corporation. It is the key economic institution of modern capitalism, but it is also the least controlled of market entities. Because corporations cannot be depended upon to act in the public interest (why should they? how would they identify it?), it is necessary, as a permanent affair, to impose public controls over corporate behavior. In the long run the Educational and Scientific Estate may convert to its values the members of the technostructures who administer corporations. In the meantime, price and profit controls are a prime necessity of inflation restraint. Inflation rises out of the existence and exercise of market power. Market power, if it can be checked at all, will be curbed by public authority.*

In 1973, actual economic policy contained elements of all the major alternatives. In the Justice Department a new antitrust chief was viewing fixed commissions on the stock exchange with a suspicious eye, as well as General Electric's reciprocal buying arrangements, IBM's dominance of the computer market, and pricing practices in autos, steel, and aluminum. The new broom, Thomas E. Kauper by name, reiterated the old faith:

The antitrust laws were passed to protect rather than destroy free enterprise. Our strongest supporters should be the business community, if for no other reason than that the alternative to antitrust is even less palatable for the nation's businessmen. For the natural next step for a cartelized economy is government ownership.†

One might argue, with moderate plausibility, that sporadic antitrust enforcement (rather than none at all) has prevented even more concentration of control than has actually occurred.

The congressional action which tied social security

*Here the crucial question concerns the capacity of giant corporations to control the controllers, as they have consistently done in the case of the regulatory agencies.
†"The Big Antitrust Crackdown," in *Dun's* (May, 1973), p. 56.

pensions to living costs and federal pay scales to private-sector labor markets implied willingness both to accept inflation as inevitable and cushion its impact, at least upon members of deserving groups. Broadened exemption of low-wage earners from controls is perhaps to be interpreted as still another instance of the same congressional attitude.

On the part of the President and his advisers, Phase II controls and even the weak and ambiguous Phase III restraints amounted to recognition, however reluctant, that concentrated market power does exist and even that something has to be done about its exercise during inflationary periods.

In the buzzing confusion of actual policy, planned recession also reappeared. In mid-1973, ascending rates of interest and practically zero growth in money supply aroused fear that by 1974 or sooner the economy would again be in recession.

Conflicts of value and evaluation generate inconsistencies of public action. In early May devoted readers of profit statistics were proclaiming 1973 a "vintage year for business."* From a different perspective, the year was nothing to boast of. Unemployment was sticking at 5 percent, and by conservative government estimates 4,400,000 persons were vainly hunting work. More realistic appraisals of the job market doubled that figure. Welfare families were harassed by more frequent surveillance, tighter eligibility standards, and actual reductions (in a time of soaring inflation) of cash benefits. The Nixon Administration planned to wind up a great many of the social services which offered benefits and some jobs to poor persons.

In short, control of inflation depends as always upon

---

*The judgment comes from Murray L. Weidenbaum, former Nixon Assistant Treasury Secretary. *Ibid.*, p. 11.

the political compromises that Presidents and Congresses make among their priorities and objectives. Like other modern societies, the United States can have as much price stability as it really wants to have and is willing to pay for, either through sacrifice of other targets of policy or alteration of important institutions and power relationships.

As we have had occasion to see, the perils of economic prophecy are so notorious that only rash souls or paid forecasters presume to date the next recession with any confidence. The inflation of profits and prices in 1973 may persist into 1974 or even 1975. Nevertheless, as Americans conduct their economic affairs, recession, whether it arrives promptly in 1974 or tarries until 1975, is the inescapable consequence of inflation. Those who purchased influence in the second Nixon Administration —conglomerate operators, oil speculators, land developers, the AFL-CIO, dairy farmers, and their colleagues —oppose effective restraints on profits, wages, executive compensation, dividends, and capital gains. After President Nixon honorably discharged his political obligations by removing Phase II controls in January, corporate profits in the first three months of 1973 registered their second biggest increase in history. It is unlikely that trade unionists and their leaders will content themselves with modest wage hikes for very long, when all around them their employers enrich themselves and food prices soar. Inequities multiply. As one indignant letter writer phrased his outrage: "There is something radically unjust about a 7% prime rate and executive compensation increases as high as 200%."*

Our current inflation is unstable as well as unfair. Although the manner of recession's inauguration is as un-

*In *Business Week* (May 26, 1973), p. 5.

certain as the moment of its beginning, there are many plausible scenarios. Renewed financial crisis among the stockbrokers might end less fortunately than the events of 1970. By the fall of that year, it is sobering to recall, McDonnell & Company had already failed; several other firms were known to be in grave difficulty; and Hayden Stone, one of the five biggest Wall Street houses, was trembling on the brink of bankruptcy. Only at the very last moment did it prove possible to consummate a merger between Hayden Stone and a better-managed enterprise.* Next time around, failure of a major firm might actually occur. In its wake, panic selling by terrified investors would guarantee other brokerage failures, the quick collapse of organized trading in financial markets, and a precipitous decline in new investment.

A less lurid scenario is equally possible. When the gap between inflationary expectations of ever larger profits and dividends and actual economic performance grows embarrassingly wide, icy tremors down the spines of investors are set off by unfavorable earnings reports issued by major corporations. The actual failure of a major conglomerate would shatter the confidence of the business and financial fraternity in sounder enterprises. Should failure be accompanied by fraud, investor suspicion and apprehension are likely to trigger a general flight from the stock market, collapse of new stock issues, and spreading public fear that bad times are at hand. As indeed, in these circumstances, they will be.

Even if spectacular failures and gaudy frauds† do not signal the end of boom and the start of recession, there comes a time in the inflationary spiral when the central

---

*See *The Second Crash*, by Charles D. Ellis (New York: Simon & Schuster, 1973).

†In the spring of 1973 the Equity Funding scandal, a saga of invented assets, nonexistent insurance policies, and imaginative computer programming, exemplified the sort of thing that happens in speculative periods.

bankers are impelled to do their thing and choke off the financial fuel upon which inflation runs. For reasons already explained, banking policy is the only weapon that remains to governments which are reluctant, by reason of both ideology and political interest, to damage the financial returns of its benefactors by imposing either effective restraints on prices and profits or higher taxes on corporate profits and large incomes.

If the Federal Reserve presides over a new credit crunch, the consequences will be familiar to Americans who recall the events of 1969 and 1970. Home mortgages will become unavailable. Loans to small businessmen will not be renewed. States and municipalities will be able to float new bond issues only on terms which impose politically unacceptable interest burdens on the taxpayers. A sufficiently savage policy of monetary pressure will check any boom and will guarantee a new recession as its successor.

Average Americans pay two prices for plutocratic government. During inflation, the principal gainers are the rich—old and new. Families of moderate income do well to keep up with the cost of living. In recent inflations, the working poor have not even been guaranteed steady employment. When monetary policy or more spectacular events halt inflation and usher in recession, those who pay the largest fees are the blacks, women, and youths who lose their jobs first, the factory workers whose overtime earnings disappear, and the small merchants most severely afflicted by credit shortage.

I have at some length argued that permanent inflation can be made tolerable by moderately inventive social policy. I am equally certain that implementation of radical antitrust would destroy the situations of entrenched market power upon which cost-push inflation builds. I also believe that permanent controls over large enterprises, professional charges, and major unions would, if equitably administered, keep inflation below dangerous levels and avert recession.

Of one thing I am most certain. In the present climate of American opinion, none of these policies is politically feasible because each of them imposes serious costs on dominant corporate, professional, university, and union interests. As noted earlier, permanent inflation running in tandem with permanent full employment threatens labor discipline and compels employers to redesign routine jobs as a way of attracting and retaining workers. Equitable controls entail smaller profits and more modest executive compensation.

What remains is recession. For the large and powerful, recession has its advantages. Marginal operators are squeezed out. Workers are frightened into lower rates of absenteeism and better behavior on the job. Trade-union militancy diminishes. The groundwork for another inflationary surge is prepared.

Thus it is fair to conclude that on all but exceptional occasions, the economic potentates who control Congress and the White House tacitly favor the present pattern of alternated boom and recession.

Until American politics dramatically change, that pattern will repeat itself.

This small volume on existing inflation is properly to be read also as an account of the prelude to a future recession.

ABOUT THE AUTHOR

ROBERT LEKACHMAN, a 1972 Guggenheim fellow, is Distinguished Professor of Economics at Herbert H. Lehman College of The City University of New York. He has also taught at Columbia University, where he earned undergraduate and graduate degrees, and more recently at the Stony Brook campus of the State University of New York. He is the author of *The Age of Keynes* and *National Income and the Public Welfare,* among other books. He has contributed to many general and scholarly periodicals.